Selling Your
IT Business

Selling Your IT Business

Valuation, Finding the Right Buyer, and Negotiating the Deal

ROBERT J. CHALFIN

WILEY

John Wiley & Sons, Inc.

Library of Congress Cataloging-in-Publication Data

Chalfin, Robert J.
   Selling your IT business : valuation, finding the right buyer, and negotiating the deal / Robert J. Chalfin.
     p. cm.
   Includes index.
   ISBN-13: 978-0-471-74076-6 (cloth)
   ISBN-10: 0-471-74076-4 (cloth)
   1. Computer software industry.   2. Computer service industry.   3. Information technology—Economic aspects. 4. Sale of business enterprises. 5. Business enterprises—Valuation. 6. Business enterprises—Purchasing. I. Title.
   HD9696.63.A2C525 2006
   338.4'70053'0688—dc22

                                                 2005019912

Printed in the United States of America

10 9 8 7 6 5 4 3 2 1

To my wife, Debbie,
my partner in life and my heart's feast

To our children, Risa and Benjamin,
who embody our wish list and keep us laughing

To my parents, Shirley and Joe,
who gave me the gift of unconditional love which allowed me to pursue my dreams.

Contents

Acknowledgments

Any book is the result of the efforts of many individuals:

Laura Brown, Elise Marton, David Moran, and Alan Rooks edited the manuscript and their suggestions and comments are sincerely appreciated and improved the book immeasurably.

Paul Gazaleh C.P.A./A.B.V., my fellow shareholder at The Chalfin Group Inc., offered ongoing encouragement, advice, and levity during the entire project. Roberta Sternthal, my executive assistant, in addition to cheerfully typing, retyping, and yet again retyping the manuscript, offered ongoing contributions throughout the writing process.

John Daus C.P.A., Herbert Lipman C.P.A., William Nagle C.P.A., Alan Rubin, Esq., David Rubin, Esq., and Michael Schaff, Esq., gave freely of their time and considerable expertise, greatly enhancing the value of the content. Bradley S. Rodos, Esq. provided guidance on the Sarbanes-Oxley Act of 2002. Robert Borghese Esq., Lecturer in Legal Studies and Entre-preneurial Management at The Wharton School, furnished many valuable recommendations that were incorporated into the manuscript, to the great benefit of the book.

A special note of thanks to Samantha Schackman, a business analyst at The Chalfin Group Inc., and Risa Chalfin, my daughter, for assisting with the research for this book.

Several professionals at John Wiley and Sons, including Natasha Andrews, Tim Burgard, Helen Cho, and Debra Manette were extremely helpful shep-herding the book through its final stages. I continue to be in awe of their talent, skill, and patience.

I would also like to acknowledge the efforts of Andre Vagliano, for graciously providing insightful commentary and suggestions and for doing so with an ever-present touch of humor.

I am indebted to all of the people who assisted me with this project.

Note to the Reader

The sample forms and agreements that are included with this book are for reference purposes only. They are intended for use as samples, not for use by parties actually contemplating a transaction. While the provisions contained in the sample forms and agreements illustrate many of the points made in the related materials, any document used by parties to a transaction or a proposed transaction should be drafted with the parties' particular positions in mind by advisors that can include lawyers, certified public accountants, and financial advisors. A general document not specifically adapted to a particular fact pattern will not provide the parties with adequate rights or protections.

IRS Circular 230 Disclosure: To ensure compliance with requirements imposed by the IRS, we inform you that any U.S. federal tax advice contained in this publication is not intended or written to be used, and cannot be used, for the purpose of (i) avoiding penalties under the Internal Revenue Code or (ii) promoting, marketing or recommending to another party any transaction or matter addressed herein.

Preface

This book is targeted to entrepreneurs and businesspeople who are considering selling their businesses. But it will also help those who serve as advisors in the acquisition process: attorneys, CPAs, intermediaries, marketers, and financial advisors. The book will also assist those who are acquiring or considering the acquisition of information technology (IT) businesses.

One paradigm has shifted: IT business owners will not want to wait until a traditional retirement age to sell. Today it is common for entrepreneurs to sell after a few years or more of operations, when the business reaches an inflection point of one sort or another and the founders want to move on to another opportunity.

Business owners who have the determination, skill, and ability to develop a business but are unfamiliar with the complexities and subtleties involved in selling it will benefit from reading this book. *Selling Your IT Business* aims to equip owners with the knowledge necessary to prepare to sell. Even if owners do not sell, the book will provide valuable advice on how to improve overall operations.

Selling Your IT Business provides an overview of the business sale process—everything from preparing for the sale, estimating a business's value, finding the right buyer, negotiating the sale, and closing the deal as well as the individual steps in the process, including preparation of the selling memorandum, maintaining confidentiality, the letter of intent, due diligence process, the contract, utilizing attorneys and CPAs, and what to do after the sale. The information is presented in a step-by-step format, carefully walking the reader through the preparation and the transaction. The book also provides samples of some of the forms that will be encountered in the sales transaction.

Selling Your IT Business helps to ensure that business owners are fully informed before and during the sale process and that they emerge from the transaction as protected as possible. The book will help the seller (and the buyer) avoid pitfalls—losing momentum, undervaluing the business, channeling scarce resources ineffectively, wasting time with an insincere buyer, inadvertently giving information to a competitor, and alienating employees, to name a few. Although the book cannot take the place of legal, accounting, and financial advisors, it provides a framework for readers to gain a complete picture of the entire sale process so that they can utilize these professionals more effectively and efficiently.

I hope you find the information in this book to be a valuable resource to guide you through a successful deal.

Robert Chalfin
November 2005

CHAPTER 1

What Buyers Are Looking For

Buyers purchase information technology (IT) businesses for many reasons. Naturally, the central rationale behind every purchase is the buyer's belief that the business will generate value in the future greater than the purchase price.

STRATEGIC MOTIVATIONS FOR POTENTIAL BUYERS

The best way to understand what your business looks like to a potential purchaser is to put yourself in his or her shoes, and in Chapter 3 we look in some detail at the different types of buyers and what motivates each of them. For now, let's take a general look at why someone might want to buy your IT business.

It may satisfy a strategic need. For example, acquiring your business may enable the buyer to operate with greater economies of scale. A buyer may also believe that your business would have good synergy with his or hers. For example, the acquirer may want to expand offerings to existing customers, and your business may provide a solution—a product, a service, or both. Solutions can take a variety of forms. Your offerings may enable the purchaser to conduct business more efficiently and/or attract more customers; your sales force, products, or services may attract more customers for the new entity. Or the acquirer may feel that the market is heading in a particular direction and your business will help achieve desired goals.

A buyer might also want to acquire your business to eliminate a competitor. (With the acquisition of one business by another, however, care should be taken that antitrust laws are not violated; the Hart–Scott–Rodino filing is one way the government, through the Federal Trade Commission and the Department of Justice, monitors acquisitions.) Purchasing a competitor does not necessarily ensure that the buyer will retain all of your customers. Some may have chosen you because they did not want to do business with your competitor. Not all acquisitions are positive. Some can be nonsynergistic, as expenses can mushroom, customers can defect, and revenue growth does not meet expectations. Furthermore, while some of the most likely potential buyers of your business are your competitors, discussions with them are potentially dangerous quite apart from antitrust concerns, since the exchange of information can result in the disclosure of confidential data.

Your business may be attractive to someone merely so they can prevent competitors from purchasing you.

As a result, you always need to analyze who will be helped the most if they purchase you and who will be hurt the most if they do not purchase you.

Your business also may offer a buyer extended geographical, market segment, or overall business expansion, and purchasing it may allow the acquirer to establish itself in a new territory or market altogether. It is true that as telephone and Internet bandwidth technology continues to improve and spread, physical distance is much less of a barrier for many kinds of businesses, but geographical and market reach still remain an important motivator in many purchase decisions.

Personal Motivations of Potential Buyers

Geography may also play a role in a buyer's personal interest in that he or she may want to live where your business operates. Your location may offer a pleasant environment, good schools, better climate, proximity to family and friends—any of a large number of compelling lifestyle or similar factors.

It could be that your company operates in a business area that interests the buyer. Perhaps the potential buyer is already involved in a related area and is looking to expand. Rather than developing an entirely new business unit or line, a businessperson will often opt to purchase a successful firm and merge it with existing operations.

During boom times, when it is difficult to attract and retain individuals with required skills, the acquisition of an IT business that already employs such people may be the compelling reason. Such acquisitions, however, do not occur only during times of talent shortages. They can also take place when a business wants to enter a market quickly, as this is more important than ever, and acquiring market share (with resulting economies of scale) continues to be a strong motivating factor.

BUSINESS ATTRIBUTES THAT ARE ATTRACTIVE TO POTENTIAL BUYERS

Regardless of the attractiveness of your business and personal motives of the purchaser, the potential purchaser will be seeking some level of business security. Buyers want assurance that your business either is stable and likely to remain so after the sale or is projected to grow and evolve into a profitable enterprise. For many if not most buyers, this translates into concern about financial performance. Some may be wondering whether the new business will perform with the desired synergy. Still others will focus their attention on the status of product development schedules. This is where the particular strengths of your business enter into the decision.

Security for the potential buyer may come in many forms—from products that work well and strong customer relationships to a predictable cash flow and a well-trained staff. Some of the key characteristics of an IT business that entice buyers are:

- A strong management team and skilled employee base who will remain in place after the sale
- Reasonably predictable financial performance, including cash flow and profits
- A diversified customer base
- Superior in-house systems, technology, and processes
- Sought after offerings—services and products
- Strong relationships with customers, lenders, and suppliers

- Respected market presence
- Perpetual focus on research and development
- Ethics

A Strong Management Team and Skilled Employee Base, Who Will Remain in the Business after the Sale

It may seem counterintuitive, but in many (perhaps most) cases, the most important asset of any IT company is its people. If a company loses its key people, the value of the business will decline. Employees are important to a business in various ways, supplying skills and commitment and working from an established relationship with the organization. Ultimately, most IT businesses are purchased for their ability to execute, and that is largely a function of their human capital. Depth of management talent is vital to the value of any business, particularly IT businesses, and because some turnover is likely after the purchase, most buyers view current management as an important component of a sound business.

It is vital for every company to have stable and well-documented relationships with its employees. For instance, reasonable noncompete, nondiversion, and confidentiality agreements with key employees and consultants will increase the value of a business. More generally, a history of low turnover, especially in the short term, is another indication that the company has good relationships with its staff.

Although there are exceptions, most people today do not spend, and do not expect to spend, their entire career at one company. Some of the drivers behind this trend include the increasing propensity of businesses to size their workforce as conditions dictate and a growing belief by many that changing jobs typically produces individual improvement and monetary rewards. Therefore, it is important to develop individuals in every organization who can assume the roles of others. Knowledge, know-how, experience, and expertise cannot be obtained or transferred quickly; staffs need time to develop, and a management team needs time to coalesce. To the extent that the members of the management team have confidence in one another (and are well-managed from above), each person can focus attention both on what he or she does best and on what is best for the company, and no one will be wasting time on redundant tasks.

It is essential that the buyer of an IT business attempt to induce your key employees to remain with the business after the sale. The more you as seller can assist in this goal, the better the chances of the sale being a success. As soon as is feasible, you might want to attempt to discuss staff inducements with the buyer: equity sharing, increased compensation, bonuses for the employees who remain, expanded responsibility, more autonomy, increased funding for projects, or a commitment to support the existing business culture. Much of your efforts in this regard will be in the form of increased dialogue with the existing employees to allay their fears of the unknown. The employees know and have a relationship with you, and initially they will have more confidence in you than in the buyer.

However, this cultivation of staff has to be balanced with the seller's need to keep the proposed sale confidential until consummated. For this reason, discussions with certain employees frequently do not occur until just before or just after the sale.

Also as soon as is feasible, the potential buyer should speak directly with your key employees to determine their future plans. Therein lies the dilemma. To the extent the potential buyer conducts due diligence, he or she may become more comfortable with the decision to acquire your company; in many cases your employees will be very impressive and enthusiastic about "their" company, and their feelings probably will be contagious and serve to increase the buyer's desire. However, with each additional person informed about the intended acquisition, the possibility rises that confidences will be broken and rumor-fed uncertainty about the business's future will spread. One of your goals during this period should be to continually monitor and allay your employees' fears.

There is no single guideline for how long it takes to develop a good management team and employee base. However, an astute buyer will attempt to gauge the quality of yours quickly.

Reasonably Predictable Financial Performance

Steady growth in revenues and earnings is a persuasive indicator of the vibrant health of a business. Although some of the hottest initial public offerings during the recent bubble involved companies with no revenues or earnings, today most must show a history of continued growth in bottom-line earnings and top-line revenues to be attractive. By doing this, companies demonstrate that recent successes are not aberrations and that future growth is likely.

It is important to realize, however, that although traditional financial analysis looks for steady growth in revenues, unit sales, gross profits and earnings, these criteria do not always strictly pertain to closely held information technology businesses. These businesses often experience development cycles followed by sales cycles that can each last for several months, often totaling more than one fiscal year. At the beginning of the development phase, and even more so as that portion of the cycle continues, sales typically lag, since clients are hesitant to purchase technology that will soon need updating. And when a new product is finally announced, there is a lag before sales are concluded and revenues are received, causing further drain on company finances. For these reasons, a 12-month profit and loss statement often cannot fully portray an IT business's health and viability. Although not generally accepted, an 18- or 24-month statement may well portray the business's position and operating cycles with more accuracy.

Regular cash flow and profits offer tremendous reassurance to a potential buyer. Profitable long-term contracts for software, hardware, and services, as well as maintenance contracts, are the best way to demonstrate value, because these revenue streams are predictable and will reduce the buyer's concerns about risk.

Prudent businesspeople want to reduce their risk whenever practical. To the extent that your business maintains a predictable cash flow and profits as a result of long-term contracts and recurring business, a potential buyer's concern is allayed, increasing your business's potential purchase price.

Well-Diversified Customer Base

A company with a broad customer base will be more attractive to a potential purchaser. If a significant percentage of your revenues and/or profits is derived from a small number of customers, no matter how impressive or steady their purchases have been, many potential buyers will be wary, because if those few customers were to disappear for some reason, or to reduce their purchases, the impact on the company would be serious. Having a well-diversified customer base is good insurance.

If your business has been able to diversify its customer base across sectors, industries, and geographic regions, its vulnerability to adverse consequences affecting a particular customer or group of customers is greatly reduced. (Interestingly, the attempt to diversify may create an inherent conflict for some IT businesses, as they frequently grow and prosper by capitalizing on expertise in a particular niche, albeit a narrow one.)

Superior In-House Systems, Technology, and Processes

One of the greatest competitive advantages your company can have is superior in-house systems, technology, and processes. They indicate that your business understands its operating environment and is focused on improving overall service levels, revenue growth, and profitability. In addition, superior in-house systems, technology and processes allow a business to operate with less need for human interaction, making it less subject to error, labor shortages, absenteeism, and other personnel problems. Superior in-house systems, technology, and processes enable a business to continually and effectively plan for the future, mine its data more effectively, offer superior customer and supplier services, and respond quickly to new opportunities. All of these attributes encourage repeat business from existing customers, making your firm more attractive and salable.

Sought After Offerings—Services and Products

Sought after offerings—services and products can offer assurance to buyers of your company's continued success. Although this fact is not always explicitly stated, when customers purchase a given IT solution, they are entering into a long-term relationship. Implicit in this relationship is the understanding that it is to their benefit for you to prosper, as growth positions your business to provide them with innovations to improve their own businesses. Moreover, customers expect your business to be available in the future to provide ongoing service, whether it is support, software fixes, repairs, updates, maintenance, and consulting or "professional services." Interestingly, it is often an IT company's latest products or services, fine-tuned and improved through ongoing iterations, that initially attract a potential buyer. Future relations aside, if your company can supply something that your competitors cannot, a potential buyer will have greater confidence in his or her future ability to meet customer expectations. Market presence and leadership—real and perceived—are of paramount importance.

Strong Relationships with Customers, Lenders, and Suppliers

Just as good relationships with managers and other employees are important, so are strong ties to customers, lenders, and suppliers. High customer-satisfaction ratings, as well as low customer turnover, are signals to a prospective buyer that your business is healthy and should continue to thrive. These traits allow a buyer to predict future demand more easily. A good relationship with a lender also has many positive ramifications. It indicates that a third party who is knowledgeable about the business is satisfied with its creditworthiness and that the business will be able to borrow funds to achieve its objectives. Finally, a business that has developed strong partnerships with suppliers typically can achieve good credit terms, minimal inventory-carrying costs, and lower overall cost of goods and operating expenses. All of these relationships improve a business's efficiency and profitability.

Respected Market Presence

An IT business with a well-respected presence and visibility in its market will be more attractive to a buyer than one with little recognition. If a buyer wants to enter a market, his or her first choice typically will be to acquire a business with strong market visibility, good brands, and a loyal customer base. All of these traits increase the chances that existing customers will continue to buy. In addition, businesses with the highest name recognition—market leaders—typically will be the first ones any buyer will consider purchasing in a particular sector or market space.

Predictable Cash Flow and Profits

Perpetual Focus on Research and Development

Because the IT world is in a constant state of evolution, it is of paramount importance that your business strives continually to improve its offerings and satisfy market and technological demands. Every solid business leverages its market knowledge to maintain competitive advantage. A business with a history and continued future likelihood of introducing new solutions, products, and services that meet the needs of the market will naturally be far more valuable than one that does not.

Of course, your business has its own strengths and unique characteristics, so it is not necessary for every factor listed to exist for your business to be desirable and seen as such. In fact, sometimes only one of these factors will make it attractive to buyers. However, the stronger your business appears—meaning the more of these factors exist—the greater the price it will command.

Ethics: A Key to Success

All businesses should be operated ethically. This high, but required, standard is of continual and paramount importance throughout a business's existence and assumes greater importance when a business is being sold. The purchaser will attempt to verify the accuracy of the representations and statements made by the seller. A buyer must have confidence in the business that is being purchased. Moreover, ethically run businesses generally have fewer issues that will cause concern to the purchaser and delay the transaction. As the purchaser's level of comfort rises, the level of perceived risk declines, which results in a higher sale price for the business. There is a very high correlation between the businesses that succeed and the ones that are operated ethically.

CHAPTER 2

Why Sell?

We have covered some of the factors that make your IT business valuable to potential buyers, and the next questions concern the sale itself:

- Why do you want to sell?
- How can you tell if your timing is right?
- What kinds of potential buyers can you expect to deal with?

REASONS FOR SELLING

Private businesses sell for a variety of reasons. Some have to do with the owner and his or her family. Perhaps the owner is ready to retire. The question then is what to do with the business. In some families, the business might be turned over via sale, gift, or inheritance to children, grandchildren, or other relatives. But when there are no capable and interested family members or relatives, the business may be sold.

Businesses also are sold because they have become unsatisfactory in some way—personally or financially. The rewards, including overall satisfaction and remuneration, may no longer be as satisfying as they once were. Perhaps the business is simply no longer exciting for the owner and running it is becoming a chore. Or the business may have reached the point where it requires more attention, skill, energy, or capital than the owner is willing or able to expend. For example, the business may be encountering increased competition, or the markets in which it operates are evolving and the owner may no longer have the personnel, capital, or other resources to contend with such changes.

Finally, if a business starts to go into a decline, an owner may decide to sell before it declines further.

Traditionally people sold businesses when they achieved certain life stages, such as retirement or disability. In today's world, a business owner should not make the decision to sell based on only these events. You should always consider your business as well as your personal and lifestyle issues.

However, businesses may also be sold while (indeed, because) they continue to perform satisfactorily. Perhaps the business is growing and its owner feels he or she does not have the ability, mettle, or resources to take it to the next level; in such a circumstance, it makes sense to let someone else assume the task. (This happens often with IT companies.) If you can sell now and reap a good price or even just minimize your ongoing risk and obligations, a sale may make a great deal of sense.

A business owner can decrease his or her involvement in the business in several ways, quite apart from an outright sale to a third party. These ways include:

- Partial sale to a third party
- Sale of all or a portion of the business to key employees
- Sale, gift, or bequeathing of all or part of the business to family members
- Hiring of competent top management, thereby decreasing your involvement while maintaining uninterrupted ownership
- Liquidating, not selling, the business

Since an initial public offering, or IPO, is typically an option for only larger businesses or those with unique, proprietary technologies, it will not be discussed in this book.

Each of the options has positive and negative attributes. Although a partial sale of the business to a third party may generate much-needed funds, the new owner(s) may demand veto power over the company's major decisions before investing in the business. This could create a problem if your vision for the business differs from the vision of the new owners. Moreover, the new owners may not want your business to expand into an area that could harm their business, such as selling to one of their competitors.

If you are the type of individual who likes to remain in control, some of these alternatives may not be viable because other people can exercise control over various aspects of your business.

WHEN SHOULD YOU SELL YOUR IT COMPANY?

When is the ideal time to sell? The brief answer is when things are going well. However, this is not always possible.

The best time to sell any business is when it is the most robust, naturally: when the business's revenues, gross margin, profits, cash flow, and customer satisfaction grow and improve on a year-to-year basis and your market share is expanding. Another good time is when the market is expanding or changing due to external factors. For example, when various industries you sell to are facing deregulation, they often must reengineer their operations and offerings immediately. Many technology vendors that serve these markets, even tangentially, will experience a rapid increase in the demand for their products—if their company's offerings satisfy these new needs. When the increased need and projected need for your products have been determined and you have shown you can meet the demand, your business's value will rise.

Another particularly good time to consider selling is when your company has just released (or is about to release) a new product that is receiving (or is expected to receive) wide acceptance and approval. The potential will attract buyers and help you realize a good price.

Always put yourself in the buyer's shoes: Who would not be attracted to a business that is likely to keep on making money? A business that is financially healthy, with good prospects, justifiably optimistic about the future, and enjoyable to run is one that is typically in good shape to sell. Potential buyers will be attracted by the sense of optimism.

To sum up, strong businesses typically:

- Attract and retain qualified employees
- Report increased earnings and revenues and a growing but manageable backlog (If the company cannot satisfy its backlog in a reasonable period of time, it can be at a disadvantage.)
- Release new, widely accepted products/services

- Continually expand their market shares
- Project growing earnings and cash flow
- Are enjoyable and exciting to operate

WHEN SHOULD YOU *NOT* SELL YOUR IT COMPANY?

Logic suggests that times of trouble are not the optimal moment for selling your business. When the business is not what it should be, it will be harder to obtain the price you want and perhaps harder to attract buyers in the first place. (For the right buyer, however, a troubled IT business can present an excellent opportunity. Opportune conditions already have been discussed, but not everyone has the luxury of being able to wait until then. Moreover, if your business can offer what the buyer seeks regardless, whether it is a product, service, or a trained workforce, it may be very desirable.) Several red flags should alert you to particularly bad times for selling:

- Your competition starts to decrease your market share, making it difficult to forecast future profitability.
- Your product is long overdue for a revision, reposition, or major upgrade and a new release is not imminent.
- You have suffered defections of key personnel and project a climate of disarray.
- You have lost key clients or customers.
- Your business is facing a period of declining revenues, profits, and cash flow.
- Your market is in decline due to external factors.
- The business no longer has a valid business model.

None of these factors or attributes is an absolute, and each may be outweighed by positives. Moreover, if you feel that these trends can be reversed, it may be beneficial to wait until the problem(s) is (are) corrected. Other red flags are discussed in Chapter 6.

Each negative occurrence may create an opportunity for potential buyers. If your company's product is long overdue for an upgrade, consolidation with another company with sufficient technical staff may enable you to develop a new product (and temporary upgrades, too) more quickly while still benefiting from your business's name, reputation, and customer base. (Moreover, the acquirer may be able to convert the users of your product to its product.) Similar logic applies if your business has a great product but insufficient personnel, working capital, or infrastructure: Its acquisition by another company may solve this deficiency. Finally, if your company is being sought chiefly for a product or personnel, any loss of key clients or market share may not be as important to a buyer as simply getting the technology or intellectual capital.

CASE STUDY

NEED TO SELL QUICKLY

Several years ago, a business owner determined during the first week of October that he wanted to sell his business by Thanksgiving of that year. He arrived at this decision after analyzing the business's short-term projections and realizing that the business would not have sufficient funds to meet its payroll beginning on December 1. While that created a very challenging task, it also crystallized many of the problems facing the business owner in today's market. In this case, the development of a new product, which could reasonably be expected to generate future sales, had taken far longer than anticipated, draining critical funds, utilizing employee resources, and seriously damaging sales in its major product line.

The business had to take a multipronged approach immediately while it sought potential buyers:

Attempt to raise cash, from investors or by borrowing.

Reduce all unnecessary expenditures.

Contact creditors and attempt to obtain additional time to pay outstanding obligations.

Develop a list of a dozen or fewer potentially interested acquirers who could be seen in the next few weeks.

Defer bonuses to several key employees.

Once you are sure about putting your business up for sale, it is time to give further thought to the other half of the process: the buyer. Choosing your buyer—to the extent that you can (see Chapter 3)—is an important decision because it is very rare for a sale to occur without the buyer and seller working together for a period of time after the transaction. It is by no means unheard of and it will probably increase the ultimate sale price if the seller continues to work as an employee for a period of time after the business is sold. Most buyers, especially those with a strategic vision, will want you to assist with the transition and typically request that you execute an employment contract for a few months after the sale (and perhaps much longer). A well-drafted contract should provide for you, as seller, to receive incentives based on the business's continued success. Although this assistance is a common request, it often proves difficult for someone who was both entrepreneur and boss to work for someone else in a usually larger and perhaps more bureaucratic environment.

The emotional contrasts during this process can be stark. During negotiations and the due diligence period on through closing, the buyer and you have divergent interests. Among other goals, the buyer wants to minimize the price while you want to maximize it. But at the moment of closing, competing interests converge—at least for the duration of your employment contract and any earn-out period. After closing, sellers usually are heavily involved in maintaining "business as usual," quelling fears or trepidation from employees, clients, or business partners while assisting in the buyer's involvement in growing and redirecting the business.

The buyer should attempt to induce you to stay and contribute, and probably will. The incentive compensation paid should be designed to encourage sellers to do what they do best, which may include:

- Attract new business
- Retain existing business
- Help improve the quality of the business's offerings
- Maintain the functionality and morale of the organization

Just as buyers should encourage sellers to stay after the sale, you should be sensitive of your new role in the business and be careful not to meddle, micromanage the new processes, impede or unintentionally sabotage, assert or reassert leadership, or otherwise overstay your welcome. You will want to be as supportive as you can bear to be. Some sellers find this period more difficult than anticipated, even when they thought they were quite ready to let go. It is the author's experience that most selling owners leave, or are forced out, within 18 months. However, in some instances selling owners thrive in the new environment. They may thrive in a large corporation, which provides them with an entry to new, larger customers; provides them with administrative support, freeing them from the tasks they deplore, such as personnel and finance; and enables them to devote their energies to what they can do best, such as research and development, marketing, or sales.

CHAPTER 3

Types of Buyers

UNDERSTANDING YOUR BUYER

Before discussing specific types of buyers, let us first review some negotiation background. Some businesspeople always expect to negotiate the price and virtually every other aspect of a deal, including such innocuous items as the time and location of meetings. These people may feel they are not doing their job unless there are extensive negotiations and concessions by the other party. Other people abhor the negotiation process. Still others are in between. To understand your buyer, it is important to analyze his or her negotiation style and continually evaluate what is important.

If you are selling to a large company or selling to someone using an intermediary, agent or representative, which could include a consultant, broker, investment banker, lawyer, or certified public accountant, it is crucial to determine the authority of the people you are dealing with. Although it is best to negotiate directly with the principals, such as the chief executive, chief operating, or chief financial officer of the acquiring entity, that is not always feasible. Generally, the more responsibility the individual has in the acquirer's organization, the more likely it is that you will know early on whether the deal will be consummated. Simply stated, these people would not invest their time unless they were seriously interested in acquiring your business.

In some instances, potential buyers are evaluating many possible acquisitions simultaneously. In such cases, representatives who have minimal decision-making authority typically make initial contacts; their job is to compile data and prepare an analysis for decision makers. Although it is important to provide these initial representatives with the data they need, keep in mind the limitations on their authority.

It is important for you, the seller, to perform due diligence on the buyer to determine his or her overall intent and method of doing business. Among the items that you are to consider are these:

- Does the buyer seem earnest about acquiring your business?

- Do the buyer's representatives appear to have the authority to recommend or approve the transaction?

- What is the buyer's negotiating style? Is it a style that you are comfortable working with?

- Is the buyer's culture complementary to your business's culture? "Culture" can include a variety of issues, from work pace, customer relations, and dress code to treatment of employees and customers.

- Will your employees be able to work for the buyer? How does the buyer treat existing employees? Interestingly, items, such as the details of the acquirer's dress code, vacation policy, and employee healthcare plans, can have a major affect on whether a transaction is successful. Items that are frequently overlooked in a transaction—deductibles, copayment amounts, prescription cards, and the like—can cause employees to be unsettled at precisely the time a transaction is announced.

FIVE KINDS OF BUYERS

There are at least five types of buyers:

1. Synergistic or strategic
2. Financial
3. Extreme bargain hunters
4. Romantics
5. Focused or cherry pickers

Synergistic or Strategic Buyers

The most desirable type of buyer wants your business for synergistic and strategic purposes. *Synergy* is the state in which the whole is greater than the sum of the parts, and in such an acquisition, the newly combined entity is more valuable than the two individual entities.

A synergistic buyer will want to purchase your business in order to:

- Satisfy strategic needs
- Obtain economies of scale
- Eliminate competition
- Expand into adjacent markets, geographic, vertical, or horizontal
- Grow the business, since the buyer has the necessary financial or managerial resources

Typically, a synergistic buyer will pay a higher price than other types of buyers, as the main goal is not simply to achieve a high return on investment from your business as a stand-alone entity. One test to determine who your most likely buyers would be is to analyze which of your competitors, customers, or suppliers would have the most to gain if they purchased your business and the most to lose if someone else bought it.

Many traditional business valuations are based on some multiple of existing income or sales or on a discounted future earnings or cash flow stream. However, if a combination with a synergistic buyer would produce a substantial boost in the new business's combined income and/or sales, your business's value will also increase. Of course, an astute synergistic buyer will not pay for all of the projected increase, as the projected rise in value is speculative and based on the new efforts.

Synergistic buyers can take several forms. *Direct competitors* may be attracted to your business because the combined entity—with increased market share—can eliminate redundant expenses and/or maximize the value of existing assets. Acquiring your company will also eliminate the costs associated with competing with it.

Alternatively, a synergistic buyer may be seeking *cross-selling opportunities*: situations in which two companies may sell different products or services to the same market or to different markets that could utilize the other's products, services, or customer bases. Combinations of similar companies that operate in the same market can create substantial cost savings and economies of scale through greater purchasing power and optimized workforce management.

A *vertical combination* occurs when a supplier purchases a customer or vice versa. *Horizontal combinations* involve companies that sell to similar but not identical customer bases. *Geographically based mergers* can occur between companies that sell to similar customer bases in different locations.

Synergy abounds in the business world. Here is one simple example of how it helped obtain the highest price for a business:

CASE STUDY

SYNERGY AT WORK

A company has income of approximately $200,000 a year after paying a reasonable salary to the owner. A recent review of the business's client list revealed that if the business's largest customer (which accounted for approximately one-third of its sales) bought the business, the customer could save $300,000 a year by consolidating all the services that it now outsources and allowing the new entity to perform them. If this customer purchased the business, it would receive benefits of $500,000 per year ($200,000 income + $300,000 savings.)

The potential disadvantage to the seller approaching such a customer is that the customer would quickly realize how important its business is to the seller's health. Such a realization would increase the purchaser's power when negotiating day-to-day pricing. This effect could be partly mitigated by the buyer's recognition of possible loss in the event that the business was sold to a competitor.

This example highlights the value of synergy and perhaps creating an auction for your company. (The process of creating an auction is discussed in Chapter 8.)

Financial Buyers

A financial buyer typically makes a decision to purchase a business based on traditional calculations such as return on investment, discounted cash flow, and return on equity and internal rate of return. For these buyers, the main factors in buying a business are the desired rate of return and assumptions and projections concerning future operating results.

Private equity investors represent one group of financial buyers. Financial buyers should be expected to pay a fair value for a business, but typically not as much as a synergistic or strategic buyer would.

Extreme Bargain Hunters

These buyers seek out troubled businesses for purchase at distressed prices. Extreme bargain hunters try to uncover businesses that are overly eager, perhaps desperate to sell. Some examples would include those with operational or cash flow problems, an ongoing feud between owners, or those whose owner is sick, recently disabled, or deceased. The price offered is typically below the price offered by the other categories of buyers.

Romantic Buyers

These buyers are attracted to a company for reasons that may not be directly related to its finances, operations, or even prospects. Romantic buyers may desire to live where the business is located, as sometimes happens with businesses in warm climates or resort areas. They may also be motivated to relocate closer to family, friends, financial backers, or customers. Alternatively, romantic buyers may be indulging a long-standing desire to operate a business in a particular sector. The IT world aside, they may have dreamed for years of running a bookstore, a restaurant, a horse farm, a newspaper, or a sports franchise, or they may want to own a business that allows them to work with those types of businesses. More likely in the IT world, romantic buyers may simply be intrigued—excited by the intellectual challenge and financial promise that your business offers or the market(s) that it serves.

Focused or Cherry Picker Buyers

Focused or cherry picker buyers may purchase a business solely for a particular attribute such as its sales force, development team, customer list, or product. This type of buyer may have no interest in any other aspect of the business and may sell, grant autonomy, or liquidate the parts of the business that are outside of its immediate focus. The price that this type of buyer may pay for the business will be dependent on the value it ascribes to the portion or component of the business it desires.

The Selling Memorandum

Once you have decided to sell your IT business, your first thought may be to line up potential buyers. However, before engaging with anyone interested in your business, you should first prepare a short description and overview of the business—a selling memorandum, or "book." A good selling memorandum paints as complete and understandable a picture as possible of the entire business, including its mission, products and services, key employees, customers, competitors, financial information, and strategic vision.

CREATING A SELLING MEMORANDUM

The business plan, with a few adjustments, can be the basis for the firm's selling memorandum. A selling memorandum or book should provide all relevant information that a potential buyer needs in order to make an informed purchase. It is one of the most important marketing documents that will ever be prepared for your business. As it will be the first item, or one of the first, read by someone seeking to buy your business, it should showcase the successes of your prior efforts to grow the business. The presentation must be professional, informative, accurate, and succinct, but it does not need to be glitzy.

The selling memorandum can be taken directly from your business plan. The remainder of this chapter discusses the preparation of the business plan.

Every business, for sale or not, should update its business plan continually. In today's rapidly changing IT world, a business plan that is more than three to four months old often is outdated. Before and during a sale, an up-to-date plan can provide you, the seller, with a distinct advantage when negotiating with a potential buyer. In addition, being able to provide a potential buyer with this book as soon as it is requested gives you a psychological advantage. If the buyer has to wait for the book, he or she may rely on less accurate projections, may contact other potential sellers, and may even lose interest in your business. The ability to supply a book on demand also demonstrates that you are well organized and view strategic planning as a vital part of achieving your goals.

As a seller, you should assume that most buyers are knowledgeable and well prepared. Typically buyers will research a business before approaching it. However, if the seller has an accurate, succinct, and sufficiently comprehensive analysis of the business and the environment in which it operates, all parties can proceed with similar information. One of the most important barriers a buyer needs to pass is feeling comfortable with your business's sales, cash flow, and profit projections. A selling book with reasonable-sounding projections, buttressed by substantiated and fair-sounding assumptions, will help allay the potential buyer's concerns. A seller who reports relatively flat historical revenues, margins, and earnings and projects rapidly increasing projected revenues, margins, and earnings the graph of which resembles a hockey stick, will encounter substantial skepticism from potential buyers. Chapter 13 discusses the dilemma that many sellers face when disclosing this information to potential buyers.

Exhibit 4.1 illustrates the typical hockey stick curve, with all of the growth occurring in the future.

WHO PREPARES THE BUSINESS PLAN?

The preparation of a business plan is a dynamic process. The exercise provides a forum for your company's key people to discuss, debate, analyze, and focus on the future while allowing for different perspectives to be considered. For these reasons, as many key employees and advisors as possible should be involved in creating the business plan. Involving while properly managing and harnessing the talents of everyone creates a stronger sense of purpose, commitment, and urgency than if one or two members of management or outsiders merely prepare a plan with a set of goals and subsequently broadcast it to the employees. The purpose and potential uses of the business plan should be communicated to the employees and those who will

EXHIBIT 4.1   HOCKEY STICK GROWTH PROJECTION

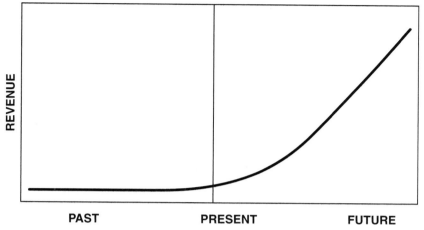

be involved in its creation. As more information about your firm's likely future is shared with management and other key individuals, all participants will become better able to understand, and perhaps help make, key decisions. What's more, everyone who helps prepare the business plan will rightly feel as if they contributed to it, becoming stakeholders and assuming a sense of pride and ownership in achieving the plan's projections and intentions.

A thorough plan should contain information obtained, synthesized, and verified from multiple perspectives. Many of your employees can provide valuable input for the business plan. Developers are aware of the strengths and weaknesses of new offerings, as well as the new technologies that are being introduced; project managers can provide insight on when new offerings will be available; customer support people know about the deficiencies in existing products; salespeople can provide an overview of the competition and the existing market; and the CFO and controller can provide information on the company's current and projected financial condition.

Everyone should be encouraged to be candid and unbiased about the business's goals—not only regarding sales projections but also regarding product completion dates and overall customer satisfaction. The business plan is much more valuable in the long run if it is accurate in these respects as well as the more usual ones.

Trade groups, customers, and suppliers can also be valuable sources of intelligence during this process. Although some businesses are reluctant to share their plans with their suppliers and customers, these entities, if properly selected and enlisted, can provide helpful, high-level, and/or targeted insight into the direction of the industry as well as the current and future needs of your business. While the information that is provided to business partners such as suppliers and customers will need to be edited, they will appreciate your efforts to plan for the future, satisfy their needs, and remain viable and growing. In today's world, many successful business relationships evolve into formal or informal partnerships: the experience of working together fosters increased awareness among the parties of their skills and strengths, which in turn fortifies the relationships these organizations have with your company.

Of course, when preparing your strategic plan, it is also important to solicit the input of your attorney, certified public accountant, banker, and investors. They can provide valuable advice from different perspectives. When they are comfortable with your business's ability to grow and meet its obligations, bankers are more likely to make further loans and investors will be more content with their investment. If investors perceive the business is performing according to plan, they may be willing to invest or lend more, will be less concerned about their investment, and may well encourage others to invest or lend money to the business. By working with a business's management team during the preparation of a business plan, the banker can witness management's talents and skills. As a result, the lender typically views the business more favorably.

Contents of a Typical Business Plan

The business plan typically includes:

- Executive summary
- Mission statement, vision, and operating principles
- Solutions offered: the business's products and services
- Marketplace
  - Customers
  - Suppliers and business partners
  - Competitors

- Management and key employees
- Company history
- Ownership and debt structure
- Lease obligations
- Changes that will occur over time and upon sale
- Business assessment and SWOT (strengths, weaknesses, opportunities, threats) analysis
- Plans for expansion
- Financial information, both historical and projected

Before discussing the various sections of the business plan, it is important to emphasize that it should be succinct, concise, and easily understandable by those who will be evaluating the business. Remember, many of the people who will be reviewing the business plan do not have a technical background and have limited time. If the plan is too complex, laypeople may not comprehend the business and envision its potential.

Executive Summary

This is a short, two- to three-page summary of the entire business plan and is typically the last section written. Often the executive summary is shown before the entire business plan or selling memorandum is distributed, as some potential buyers may not agree to execute a confidentiality agreement until they review the executive summary. As a result, it should not contain information that is deemed to be confidential.

Mission Statement, Vision, and Operating Principles

Your business may or may not have these items already prepared. In any case, now is a good time to start crafting and updating them. A vision statement typically discusses the broad objectives of your business and how you see them evolving in the future. A mission statement, if separate, provides a road map of how your business will achieve its vision. Operating principles are the business practices and ethics that are important to your company. As with the business plan, the creation of these documents should involve many different people and departments within your organization.

Solutions Offered

This section should discuss the solutions—both products and services—offered by your business. It should elaborate on the ways the business assists its clients and might mention the company's pricing strategies and profit margins. Because many readers may not be conversant with your business's intricacies, this information must be lucid and readily understandable. Remember, people are more apt to invest in, lend to, or purchase a business if they clearly understand what it does. The book should summarize the value of utilizing your business to prospective customers, which, apart from your products and services themselves, can be increased efficiency, cost savings, or better service.

EXHIBIT 4.2   SUPPLIERS CUSTOMERS AND COMPETITORS

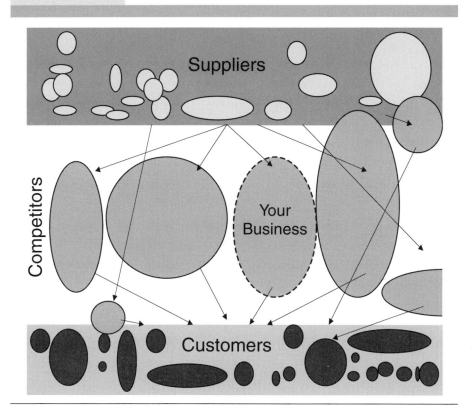

Your Marketplace

This section is often intertwined with the solutions section. It should discuss your business's customer base and the areas in which your market can be expected to evolve, expand, or contract. Exhibit 4.2 provides an illustration of the marketplace.

The discussion of your cusotmers should also include an analysis of potential specific future customers as well as detailed analysis of the size, breadth, and potential of the marketplace(s) where you currently sell your solutions. Because most business owners do not realize how large their market is, this is probably one of the most difficult—but most important—sections to prepare with substantiation and accuracy. However, it must not be prepared in a manner that causes the buyer to view the projections as unrealistic.

Customers   Most potential buyers are keenly interested in your customer base, particularly the most profitable customers or clients. One key element of this section should be the extent of your business's dependence on key clients. For example, your business plan should answer how many clients account for 10 or 20 percent of the business's sales and what portion of the total sales the largest 5 or 10 customers account for. Also, top-tier or marquee clients that are easily recognized should be identified, since they may add substantial credibility to your pitch.

In addition to learning about current customers, a potential purchaser will want to know how your company generates new business. The length of your sales cycle—the time from contact to contract—should also be described and discussed. Concomitantly, the revenue cycle—which is the time from when the services are performed or products are delivered and payment is received—should be highlighted. The plan should analyze the processes and means used to attract new customers. This analysis can include discussion of lead generation and qualification, as well as the specifics of the value propositions your business offers, such as lower pricing, better service, increased efficiency, integration with other offerings, disintermediation (direct selling, cutting out middlemen), or other added values. The business's estimated or projected marketing and advertising budgets should be discussed as well.

Suppliers and Business Partners   Supplier or partner relationships with other companies can be very important assets as well as potential liabilities.

For example, if your business resells another company's hardware, software, or services, details about these relationships, including markets or territories served, margins, obligations, length of relationship and likelihood of renewal, should be provided. The likelihood that such relationships will grow, contract, or be severed should be discussed, along with any changes that may occur in margins or payment terms. You should also focus on the financial strength of these partners along with the switching costs that could be incurred to replace them. These relationships can be viewed as a liability if the potential buyer is loath to enter into a relationship with them. Conversely they can be an attraction to an acquirer who would otherwise not be able to enter into relationships with these partners and suppliers.

Competitors   Analysis of competition is as important as any other factor in the sales pitch. Believe it or not, when asked to name their competitors, small-business owners frequently reply, "We have none," or they fail to properly acknowledge the presence of all of their existing as well as potentially formidable competitors. In reality, in today's global business village, your business's competitors can be drawn from far and wide. Accordingly, it is important to assess and evaluate any and all competitors, current and potential.

Although difficult to forecast, the potential for future competitors should also be included in a business plan. Consider everyone who provides or could provide the same solution as current competitors or could solve your customers' problem via alternative means. (You might consider withholding information on this topic until a buyer's interest is confirmed.)

Keep in mind that another form of competition is the customer who decides not to purchase a solution from anyone and instead attempts to develop it in-house. Although every business grapples with strategies on how to transform such potential customers into actual customers, in this section it may be helpful to consider them as potential competitors or as a cause for reduced revenue projections.

Management and Employees

In any IT business, human capital is absolutely vital. Among the myths surrounding the sale of IT businesses is that, after a company is sold, the new owners will invariably lay off good people. This statement is inaccurate in many situations. Many IT businesses are purchased for their workforce as well as for their current and potential software applications or services. This includes research and development (R&D), marketing, support, sales, administrative, and executive personnel. An astute purchaser typically wants to retain experienced people and designs and maintains employee compensation and other plans to achieve that goal.

Savvy investors have even been known to choose a company with great management and only good technology over a company with great technology and only good management. The difference that can propel an IT business to new heights is superior management coupled with an attractive employee base. A salient consideration for every potential business purchaser, therefore, is the composition of your business's management and its organizational structure. Every selling book should include a discussion of employee experience as well as an up-to-date organizational chart. Detailed work biographies of key personnel can be included in an appendix as opposed to the text. The book also should briefly discuss employee retention programs and compensation plans. (This latter component is analyzed in detail in Chapter 5.)

Company History

Your company's origins and evolution are often relevant. If the business plan is organized somewhat chronologically, a brief company history should appear early on. Although this is one section you and any other founders of the business may be particularly proud of, and the source of stories and jokes, its content is less important than the sections already discussed and care should be taken to include only relevant and salient information. Delete war stories unless they are succinct and pertinent. Let your marketing and communications staff edit this section as heavily as necessary, without significant veto.

Ownership and Debt Structure

You and other owners of your company ultimately will be required to approve (or reject) the sale of the business, so a clear description of the ownership structure is vital. Almost any potential buyer will want to know this. Each business has its own bylaws and/or operating agreements governing its sale. From the buyer's perspective, the larger and more complex the ownership base, the more involved the approval process will be. However, when there are multiple owners, a lone holdout will have less of a chance of vetoing the sale, unless your business's bylaws grant a minority shareholder some form of supermajority rights or the shareholder is the majority or controlling owner of the business.

In certain instances, where the sales proceeds will not be received in cash at the closing, lenders, as well as other preferred shareholders and creditors, may possess practical, if not actual, veto rights over the proposed sale. Similar consideration should be given to the rights of stock option holders.

The ownership section should also discuss whether such creditors as bondholders or lenders have any warrants, options, or rights to convert their debt to equity. A common covenant in many loan agreements is a "due on sale" provision, requiring the debt to be paid if the business or a defined portion of it is bought. Some such provisions also provide an alternative whereby the lender must approve of the new owner to prevent the loan from becoming due. The buyer will want to review your debt structure carefully for a variety of reasons. If there is significant debt, the likelihood and practicality of an installment sale is lower, because the existence of debt that must be paid off at closing increases your cash requirements at that time. And where the cash at closing will not liquidate outstanding debt, debt holders should be apprised of the benefits of the sale as soon as is feasible as they may be agreeable to extending the loan to the new owners of the business.

Leases

The terms of your business's leases of all real estate and equipment should be provided. If the company leases one or more of its facilities from related parties, such as shareholders, that information should be discussed.

Related parties may offer more flexibility and opportunities at the time of sale. For example, lease terms may be changed and rent adjusted to market value, resulting in reduced or perhaps additional payments or other benefits to the owner. However, third-party lessors may require approval before any lease is assigned. Frequently the third-party landlords or lessors will require additional payments upon assignment to transfer the lease and subsequently on an ongoing basis. They may ask for this money to "cover" their legal fees or effectively increase the rent to market rates.

Changes That Will Occur upon Sale

If your business will experience certain changes at the time of sale, that information should be provided. Some of the more common changes revolve around the business's expenses. For example, the salaries paid to key people could increase or decrease. The amounts paid to suppliers could also change. These amounts could rise if the supplier is able to increase prices as a result of the transfer of ownership or other factors and could fall if the new buyer can negotiate better prices as a result of its increased volume and buying power.

Business Assessment or SWOT Analysis

An important opportunity afforded by the creation of the selling book is the critical evaluation of your company's current and future performance. A common assessment takes the form of a SWOT (strengths, weaknesses, opportunities, and threats) analysis. The first two components review your company from an internal perspective; the last two review it from an external perspective.

Exhibit 4.3 is a sample SWOT analysis for a software firm that also sells hardware.

EXHIBIT 4.3	SAMPLE SWOT (STRENGTHS, WEAKNESSES, OPPORTUNITIES, AND THREATS) ANALYSIS

Strengths

Customer Loyalty: With the exception of our customers who were acquired, we have retained over 95 percent of our customers over the past five years. Only rarely do we lose an existing client to a competitor.

Customers: Our clients are extremely stable, predictable, and are typically in a strong financial condition.

Reputation: Since our business was formed xx years ago, we have built a reputation for quality products and services in our industry. We have excellent references from our customers. We have received several awards from our suppliers.

Employees: One of the reasons why our customers have continued to select us is our well-trained employees. We know the importance of having talented professionals from diverse backgrounds on our staff.

In the past xx years, we have added approximately xxx staff members and independent contractors.

(continues)

EXHIBIT 4.3   CONTINUED

Multiple Software Platforms: Our software operates on these platforms: _____, _____, and _____.

Supplier Relationship: From our relationship with our suppliers, we benefit from marketing assistance and technical training. We have been the highest-level business partner since 199x. This designation allows us to obtain better pricing, training, technical support, and sales leads.

Facility: We have an impressive facility.

Financial Status: Over the past five years, our sales and profits have grown at compounded annual growth rates of ____ percent and ____ percent respectively.

Borrowing: We maintain excellent relations with our lender, ABC Bank.

Product Line: Our product suite, which consists of over _____ separate software modules, addresses most of the specific information needs of our customers.

IP Ownership: Although all of our software products are based on open industry standards and accepted platforms, the individual applications and routines were written by and are wholly owned by us.

Weaknesses

Cost for Small Businesses: For businesses with sales below $$$$$, our pricing for our solutions, which consist of hardware, software, and implementation services, is higher than many competitive existing offerings.

Telephone Support: Our telephone support is not as robust and extensive as that of our larger competitors.

Online Literature and Demonstration Materials: Much of the sales and marketing material, as well as our Web site, needs to be updated regularly to accurately reflect our ever-changing product lines.

Company Size: As we expand our client base into larger businesses, we still are perceived as being too small of a company to service big accounts.

EXHIBIT 4.3   CONTINUED

Opportunities

Strategic Alliances: Developing additional strategic alliances, such as those with
_____, _____, and _____, can provide us with additional opportunities to increase our revenues.

New Technology: Our installed base represents a large opportunity for selling these new technologies: _____, _____, and _____.

Expand to Other Markets: We have a solid product line and our offerings can be easily converted and utilized in the following industries _____, _____ and _____.

Reduction of Installation/Training Time: If we could reduce these costs it would make our product much more competitive.

Additional Services: Clients within the xxxx market may be willing to pay for consulting and other services. We need to harness the existing skills of our employees and hire new employees when appropriate to support these services.

Current Clients: Customers already within our client base provide us with an outstanding opportunity to sell additional products and services. We could increase revenues substantially by . . . .

Outsourcing: The possibility of transferring some of our functions to lower-cost countries can provide us with substantial cost savings.

Threats

Outsourcing: The current trend of outsourcing certain functions, such as development, support, and testing to India and other lower-cost countries, may enable some of our competitors to lower their costs significantly and compete with us more effectively.

Competitors: The possibility of one of our competitors acquiring another of our competitors is a serious threat. A consolidation would create a few companies that could dominate our market.

Inability to Hire Qualified Employees: If we are unable to attract, retain, and train employees, our competitors will seize upon this void.

Inability to Seize the Opportunity: We are currently in the enviable position of having the applications the market is demanding. If we are unable to grow the company quickly enough to take advantage of this extraordinary opportunity, one of our competitors may.

Plans For Expansion

You should discuss your business's plans for expansion over the next few years. Expansion can include updated or new offerings, acquisitions, entry into different markets, opening of additional or larger offices and facilities, and hiring more employees. The resources that will be required to expand the business along with the sources, revenues, and expenses should also be outlined. While this section may be initially withheld from a suitor until its interest is confirmed, this presents an opportunity to discuss the business's future with a potential buyer.

Financial Results

You should include your business's financial results for at least the three preceding years in the financial statements. Assuming the business has been in existence, the financial results for a longer period, such as 5 to 10 years, are generally preferred by buyers. In addition, any year-to-date results since the last financial statements were issued should be provided. This is one area in which the business plan should be updated continually. There should be a lag of no more than 45 days between the date the selling memorandum is provided and the last date of the financial results. When providing historical financial statements, you should explain the reasons for any aberrations, changes, trends, or anomalies. For example, new product introductions, macroeconomic events, or industry-specific factors can have a profound effect on any line-by-line year-to-year comparisons.

Also include forecasts for the next two to three years. Break out the data for the next year or two quarterly; beyond that, annually. All of these projections need to be reasonable and well considered, their assumptions clearly explained with appropriate exculpatory language that you are not predicting results.

Remember, you and your business will lose a great deal of credibility if projections are not achieved. Negotiations for the sale of a business, from the initial contact through the closing, can span many months or longer, and a potential buyer can determine whether your projections are being achieved in the first few months after receiving the business plan. If they are not, you should provide the buyer with the reasons for this before being asked.

However, the importance of providing realistic and achievable projections cannot be overstated. Whether caused by product delays, overly optimistic sales forecasts, or excess expenditures, missed projections can cause the potential buyer to look askance at all other data you provide and representations that you make.

CHAPTER 5

Attracting and Retaining Key People

$\mathcal{J}$ust as a traditional old-economy manufacturer, wholesaler, or transportation company carefully maintains its machinery and equipment while continually modernizing its facility, so must an information technology firm continually strive to attract and retain key people. Potential employees are attracted to a business for a variety of reasons, including the type of work performed, general working conditions and environment, location, benefits, compensation plans, and perquisites.

COMPENSATION PLAN OBJECTIVES

For your business's compensation plan to be effective, it should meet these objectives:

- *Equitable:* Not only should the plan be equitable, but it also must be perceived by the employees as equitable. The individual employees should feel they are being adequately compensated for their work as compared both with the marketplace and with other employees in the company.

- *Efficient:* For a plan to be effective, it must be easily and efficiently administered.

- *Understandable:* For a compensation plan to achieve its goals, it must be easily understood by the employees. The plan should not be too complicated or require an inordinate amount of time for each employee to calculate the benefits provided.

- *Short-term and long-term goals:* All plans must be designed to align employees' goals with the business's goals. On a short-term basis, the business may desire to have its profits, cash flow, and revenues increase. On a long-term basis, it may desire that all three of these measurements grow; however, to sustain long-term growth, the business should also focus on how its customers rate the quality of its offerings and service. If customers continually approve of the quality of services, which will probably be at least in part a function of your employees' behavior, this increases the likelihood of increased, repeat, and referral business.

- *Incentive-based:* All compensation plans should include an incentive component. Although every employee should receive a reasonable base salary or guaranteed compensation, a portion of every individual's remuneration should be incentive-based. It is this author's opinion that anywhere from 10 to 50 percent of an employee's compensation should be so based. (For certain salespeople, this percentage should be higher.) The incentive should be tied to the work and results of the individual, the unit in which the individual works, and companywide results. As the individual's responsibility grows, the portion of his or her compensation that is incentive-based should be increased commensurately.

- *Measurements and metrics:* When you design the incentive-based components of compensation plans, the metrics utilized to determine an individual's incentive-based compensation should be appropriate to align both the employees' and company's interests.

- *Reasonably attainable, in part:* A portion of the incentive-based bonus should be reasonably attainable by all employees if they achieve certain objectives and should not be perceived as being unattainable. However, the incentive-based component should not be allowed to evolve into an expectation or entitlement that it will be received regardless of the employee's and business's performance. Moreover, another portion of the incentive-based compensation should be achieved only when extraordinary results are obtained.

- *Controllable:* An incentive-based bonus should be based on objectives within the employee's control. All employees must perceive that they have the ability to affect their own incentive-based bonus. If the organization is very large, it is advisable to make a portion of compensation dependent on the results of the individual or his or her smaller unit. The motivational aspects of the plan will be lost if individuals feel they cannot affect their bonus or its size because it is based on the results of a very large organization. If the bonus is based on group results, the author has found it beneficial for the group to be no larger than 10 people and preferably no more than 6. If the group is too large, the employees may feel as if they have minimal control over their group's performance.

- *Frequent payments:* An incentive-based plan should provide for some payments that are made more frequently than once a year. In this way your employees have ongoing, perhaps quarterly, goals as opposed to one goal that may appear remote or distant.

- *Vesting requirements:* Your compensation plan should also be designed to retain good people. As a result, appropriate vesting and service requirements should be instituted to encourage employees to remain with the company for a period of time before they are able to receive the components of the deferred compensation. These vesting requirements are another method for achieving the business's goals. If the goal is to retain a key person for a fixed period of time, his or her benefits should vest coincident with that time period. If the business's goal is to be sold at some point, the benefits should vest at the time of the sale, or preferably afterward, in order to provide the key employees with incentives to work with the new owner even for a short period. This will ease the transition.

- *Employee involvement:* As many of your employees as possible should be involved in designing the plan, or its components, for several reasons:

  - Employees will understand, from their direct involvement, the underlying complexities as well as the cost of the plans, including the challenges of satisfying the various constituencies.

  - It will enable the plans to be designed to more closely fit the needs of individual employees.

  - The employees who assisted in designing the plan will become advocates and liaisons between management and their fellow workers and can discuss and promote the new initiatives and suggest changes or modifications where appropriate.

- *Right to change:* The employer should always retain the right to change, alter, amend, increase, or decrease the plan or its provisions for any or no reason. However, whenever a plan is changed, the reasons should be clearly communicated to your employees. Appropriate reasons for changing a plan could be that it is ineffective or that the company does not have the financial resources to continue. (Of course, you should never decrease or reduce any employee's vested benefit.)

- *Communicated to employees:* For a plan to be effective, it must be communicated with the employee participants clearly and regularly. Frequent communication enables the employees to understand and appreciate its personal value. There are numerous instances of knowledgeable employees not being fully aware of the scope and extent of their potential compensation rewards, which defeats any motivational benefits. Communicating a plan to your employees only once, or even once a year, is not sufficient. The plan should be communicated several times a year. The form of communication should take many different forms: individual meetings, group meetings to discuss the plan (not data specific to individual employees), written summaries, and plan documents handed out.

In an entrepreneurial business, it is important that all employees feel they can directly affect results and concomitantly their remuneration. One method for spreading some of the entrepreneurial spirit is to make every employee at every level responsible for the achievement of your company goals. Under this plan, the employees will benefit if through their efforts the business does well; conversely, their compensation will suffer if the results are not as strong as were expected. Another advantage of officially encouraging, and monetarily incentivising, every employee to be responsible for specific or business-wide results is that it reduces the need to manage individuals. When appropriately selected, employees who have properly designed compensation plans will be motivated to be both resourceful and diligent in achieving individual goals that are aligned with the overall goals.

Another advantage of designing appropriate incentive-based compensation plans is that it can reduce your company's cash flow requirements during periods when collections are slow or cash flow is tight, as when your business is growing its customer base and/or employee population. In many IT firms, personnel and personnel-related costs frequently account for two-thirds or more of total expenditures. A properly designed incentive compensation plan can reduce these costs by 10 to 15 percent or more during times when cash flow is tight, and this can have a meaningful affect on a business's viability.

QUICK TIP

One of the reasons businesses enter into budgeting processes, of course, is to attempt to determine if they will have sufficient cash flow to fund their operations. A compensation plan that increases employee payouts during robust times and decreases them during lean times will reduce the business's reliance on a budget to sustain its operations.

More traditional compensation plans frequently include base salary plus bonus. The bonus typically is based on the achievement of predetermined goals by the individual, the individual's working unit, and/or the company overall. All bonus plans should attempt to influence both short-term and long-term results. Bonuses can be tied to metrics such as profits, gross margin, market share, expense reduction, and revenue growth. However, using historical results as the sole basis for determining bonuses does not encourage the employees to build the value of the business for the future as opposed to merely increasing the historical measures for their own short-term gains. Although bonuses based on historical performance, or an average of the results of several years, may appropriately motivate employees, this author believes that bonuses should be instituted in tandem with other "future-based" plans.

One example of a future-oriented plan is a bonus based on the overall product or service quality rating by customers. The logic behind making a bonus dependent on the company's quality rating is that if the customers are content with the company's offerings, additional business will be generated by existing customers making subsequent purchases, by their referring new customers to the business, or by their serving as references to independently prospected new customers.

QUICK TIP

A sale to an existing customer is usually more profitable than one to a new customer because the business does not have to incur the cost and investment usually required to generate a sale from a new customer. It usually is far easier to predict the purchasing patterns of existing customers, enabling the company to optimize its resources.

Equity-Sharing Plans

You, the owner, should be continually mindful about the steps you can take to retain key employees, not only through the date of closing but subsequent to the sale. Equity-sharing plans, which can take a variety of forms, can assist in accomplishing this goal. This section highlights some of the various alternatives that are available.

This book is not intended to provide an analysis of the legal, tax, or accounting ramifications affecting these various plans. The business owner is strongly urged to seek competent legal, tax, and accounting advice for a more comprehensive analysis.

When properly designed, equity-sharing programs that are offered to your key employees can serve as an incentive for them to increase the value of the business and profit when it is sold (if they are still employed by the business).

Equity-sharing plans can also play a crucial role by encouraging future employee behavior that would be beneficial to your business. Some of the more popular equity-sharing plans include stock options, stock appreciation rights, phantom stock grants, and grants of restricted stock.

Stock Options

Even though many companies have been criticized for awarding excessive stock options, there still can be a place for them in privately held businesses.

When an employee receives stock options, everyone—including you, the business owner—should remain mindful that such options might enable the employee to become an owner, albeit a minority owner, of the business in the future.

Stock Appreciation Rights and Phantom Shares

Other plans, such as stock appreciation rights and phantom stock, enable employees to share in the business's appreciation of value without becoming shareholders. Stock appreciation rights plans allow employees to receive a bonus on the appreciation of a predetermined number of stock units, whose price is tied to the company's stock. Phantom stock plans allow employees to receive a bonus based on the entire value of a predetermined number of stock units whose price is also tied to the company's stock. Both the stock appreciation rights and phantom stock bonuses usually are structured so they are taxed to the employees as ordinary income.

Restricted Stock Awards

The company can also give or award restricted stock to employees. The provisions of the restricted stock award can limit the vesting and subsequent sale of the restricted shares to a predetermined date or the occurrence of a particular event, such as the sale of the business, or a period of time, such as five to ten years.

QUICK TIP

When designing equity-sharing plans, you should consider the behavior or actions you are trying to foster and the goals being sought. For example, if one goal of the plan is to allow the employees to benefit in the event the company is sold, the stock, stock options, stock appreciation rights, or phantom stock can be granted to the employees with the provision that they do not vest until or after all, or substantially all, of the business is sold. Instituting this provision may avoid the problems of being forced to buy back employee stock when the employees leave the business before a sale, and it encourages the employees to remain and contribute until the business is sold. However, in the event the business undergoes periods of disappointing results, this plan can be harmful, as many of your key employees may leave since they may feel the business will not be sold in the foreseeable future and their options will be worthless ("under water").

Whenever employees receive an equity interest in a business, regardless of the legal form, it is prudent for your company to require them to sign a shareholder's agreement and an employment agreement. (Employment agreements are discussed in the next section.) The shareholder's agreement should provide for various contingencies including any purchase or buyback rights (of either employer or employee), the right to transfer the stock in the future, right of first refusal of the employer to buy the stock before it is sold to a third party, the right to buy back the stock, vesting, a prohibition against competing with the employer and encouraging other employees to leave your business, and others.

Employment Agreements

All key employees, if they have not already done so, should also sign an employment agreement before receiving an equity ownership interest that will govern the terms of their future employment with the business as well as any covenants or agreements that govern post employment rights and obligations. Some examples include promises not to solicit business, to the extent they are not provided for in other agreements, and the remedies if the parties do not comply.

Subject to the applicability of pertinent laws, you should consider requiring all employees, particularly key employees such as officers, managers, salespeople, and research and development personnel, to sign noncompete, nonsolicitation, and confidentiality agreements that prevent them from using your business's trade secrets, knowledge, and contacts they have gained at your business for the benefit of a competitor, whether it is a subsequent employer or a business in which they have an equity interest. These same people should also be prohibited, or at least discouraged, from inducing or encouraging former colleagues and clients from leaving your business to work for or do business with them. These provisions should be included in the shareholder's and employment agreements.

The optimum time to have the employees execute an employment agreement is when they are offered employment with your firm. Subject once again to applicable law, whenever individuals are given an offer of employment, the offer letter—which the employee should sign acknowledging his or her agreement—or the employment contract/agreement should not only state remuneration, term of employment, and any severance package but also the specific terms of the noncompete, nonsolicitation, nondiversion, and confidentiality agreements.

In certain jurisdictions this agreement may not be enforceable if *existing* employees are required to sign it as a condition of continued employment. In other situations such agreements may not be enforceable under any circumstances. However, if your business has existing employees who do not have noncompete and nondiversion agreements, one strategy, and subject to appropriate laws, is to require employees to sign the agreement in return for an equity interest in the business. In this way, the employees may be deemed to have received consideration for their agreement not to compete.

A business that has favorable contracts and agreements that prevent employees from diverting clients and customers from it is more valuable than a business that does not. As the laws in each state differ widely, you should always consult with an attorney who is thoroughly familiar with the applicable federal, state, and local laws and customs that govern employment, labor, and business competition as well as related areas.

Generally, if the prospective employee is encouraged to take the opportunity to discuss the letter's terms with an attorney, it is more likely to be enforceable than otherwise. (It is suggested that employees should never be required to sign any such agreement without being advised in writing and afforded an opportunity to review it with an attorney and financial advisor.)

CASE STUDY

LOSS IN VALUE OVERNIGHT

An owner was contemplating selling her business, which she had built for the past 15 years. It was determined that four of the seven likely buyers were local. Just as the owner was preparing to have an intermediary contact these potential buyers, the salesperson who accounted for over half of the business's revenues announced he had accepted an offer to work for the largest competitor in a similar capacity. With that announcement, substantial portions of the business's revenues, profits, and cash flow were at risk, and overnight the value of the business dropped precipitously.

CHAPTER 6

Financial Metrics

Peope use many different criteria to monitor and analyze businesses. Some are subjective, including the owners' and/or buyer's sense or feel about the projected demand for offerings, the efficiency of operations, and the perceived quality or threat of competitors' offerings.

Other, more objective results can be gauged and monitored by the use of metrics or financial ratios.

The value of any metric or group of metrics can be increased through careful monitoring of the quality and accuracy of the underlying data coupled with improved reporting systems that enable the data to be provided in a timely manner. The failure of any business to produce timely and accurate data will decrease the utility and value of any resulting metrics and the quality of the decisions made.

FINANCIAL RATIOS

A number of financial ratios have been developed specifically to gauge the performance of information technology firms. Although no single ratio or measurement provides a fully accurate assessment of a business, the metrics discussed can assist you in managing, operating, and improving your business. These definitions are used:

- *Adjusted Net Revenues:* Sales of software and services plus net sales from any item or service such as hardware or software that is purchased from another entity and resold by the business

- *Net Hardware Sales:* Gross margin from hardware purchased from a third party.
- *Net Software Sales:* Gross margin from software purchased from a third party.
- *Monthly Sustenance Level (MSL):* Payroll, taxes, insurance, rent, utilities, telephone, debt service, and other fixed expenditures that are incurred each month.
- *Personnel Costs:* Payroll, payroll taxes, health insurance, and direct employee costs. If the business uses independent contractors in place of employees and these people would appear to be employees to an outsider, the costs associated with these contractors should be included as personnel costs. Recruiting fees and hiring bonuses should also be included in this category.

The company's metrics should be reviewed over a multiyear period because results for a one- or two-year period can be skewed either positively or negatively by aberrations or temporary changes, such as the loss or acquisition of a few large clients, variations in expenditures, or the business devoting or not devoting its energies to developing new offerings. Ratios are most helpful when they are reviewed and analyzed for trends and patterns.

Profitability Ratios

Some of the traditional profitability ratios include:

$$\text{Return on Total Assets} = \frac{\text{Net Profit after Taxes}}{\text{Total Assets}}$$

$$\text{Return on Equity} = \frac{\text{Net Profit after Taxes}}{\text{Equity}}$$

$$\text{Return on Sales} = \frac{\text{Net Profit after Taxes}}{\text{Sales}}$$

Working Capital Ratios

Working capital represents current assets less current liabilities. Current assets are cash, accounts receivable, work-in-process, inventory, and all other assets that are expected to be converted into cash within a year. Current liabilities are all the liabilities of the business that are due within a year. Current liabilities typically include accounts payable, accruals, taxes payable, and the portion of long-term loans that are due within the next 12 months.

Working capital is the fuel that a business needs to sustain itself and fund its ongoing expenses, such as salaries, rent, taxes, utilities, and purchases from its suppliers. Without sufficient working capital, a business cannot survive and grow.

Some of the related working capital ratios include:

$$\text{Current Ratio} = \frac{\text{Current Assets}}{\text{Current Liabilities}}$$

$$\text{Quick Ratio} = \frac{\text{Current Assets} - \text{Inventory}}{\text{Current Liabilities}}$$

Other Ratios

The preceding ratios, along with the standard leverage and activity ratios, may not always provide a complete picture of an IT business's performance. Some other ratios that should be utilized in addition include:

$$\text{Sales per Employee} = \frac{\text{Adjusted Net Revenues}}{\text{Equivalent Full-time Employees}}$$

$$\text{Personnel Cost Ratio} = \frac{\text{Personnel Costs}}{\text{Adjusted Net Revenues}}$$

$$\text{Personnel Productivity Ratio} = \frac{\text{Adjusted Net Revenues}}{\text{Personnel Costs}}$$

$$\text{Hardware Revenue Ratio} = \frac{\text{Net Hardware Sales}}{\text{Adjusted Net Revenues}}$$

$$\text{Third-Party Revenue Ratio} = \frac{\text{Adjusted Net Revenues from the Sale of Third-Party Solutions}}{\text{Adjusted Net Revenues}}$$

$$\text{Existing-Client Revenue Ratio} = \frac{\text{Adjusted Net Revenues from Existing Clients}}{\text{Adjusted Net Revenues}}$$

$$\text{New-Client Revenue Ratio} = \frac{\text{Adjusted Net Revenues from New Clients}}{\text{Adjusted Net Revenues}}$$

$$\text{Maintenance Revenues Ratio} = \frac{\text{Adjusted Net Revenues from Maintenance}}{\text{Adjusted Net Revenues}}$$

$$\text{Software Revenues Ratio} = \frac{\text{Adjusted Net Revenues from Software}}{\text{Adjusted Net Revenues}}$$

$$\text{Service Revenues Ratio} = \frac{\text{Adjusted Net Revenues from Services}}{\text{Adjusted Net Revenues}}$$

$$\text{Large-Client Dependency Ratio} = \frac{\text{Adjusted Net Revenues from Largest Clients}}{\text{Adjusted Net Revenues}}$$

$$\text{Monthly Sustenance Ratio} = \frac{\text{Monthly Sustenance Level (MSL)}}{\text{Monthly Adjusted Net Revenues}}$$

$$\text{Discretionary Payroll Ratio} = \frac{\text{Incentive-Based Personnel Costs}}{\text{Personnel Costs Exclusive of Incentive-Based Compensation}}$$

$$\text{Fast MSL Coverage} = \frac{\text{Cash}}{\text{Monthly Sustenance Level}}$$

$$\text{MSL Coverage} = \frac{\text{Cash + Accounts Receivable to Be Collected in 30 Days}}{\text{Monthly Sustenance Level}}$$

$$\text{Prepaid Cash} = \text{Cash} - \text{Client Deposits (Prepayments)}$$

$$\text{Prepaid Liquidity} = \text{Cash} + \text{Accounts Receivable} - \text{Client Deposits (Prepayments or Unearned Revenues)}$$

$$\text{Employee Utilization (hours)} = \frac{\text{Hours Billed}}{\text{Hours Worked}}$$

$$\text{Employee Utilization (dollars)} = \frac{\text{Revenues Generated}}{\text{Employee's Compensation}}$$

$$\text{Administrative Employee Cost Ratio} = \frac{\text{Administrative Personnel Costs}}{\text{Total Personnel Costs}}$$

$$\text{Client Acquisition Costs} = \frac{\text{Costs of Obtaining New Clients}}{\text{Gross Margin}}$$

The remainder of this chapter discusses these ratios in some detail as well as some suggested internal management reports that every IT business should prepare.

Sales per Employee

$$\text{Sales per Employee} = \frac{\text{Adjusted Net Revenues}}{\text{Equivalent Full-time Employees}}$$

A profitable business should have a sales-per-employee ratio higher than its average total remuneration per employee. An employee's remuneration includes all direct payments made to or on behalf of an employee. This includes salaries, bonuses, payroll taxes, employee benefits, and perquisites. The ratio of the business's adjusted net revenues to its equivalent full-time employees is a vital metric for any IT business. A business's adjusted net revenues are equivalent to its gross revenues less the cost of any third-party hardware or third-party software that is resold.

The equivalent full-time employee measurement is used rather than the number of employees, since this measurement allows for the inclusion of part-time employees, who are converted to an equivalent full-time number.

QUICK TIP

If one employee works 60 percent of the time, that person should be considered as 60 percent of a full-time employee. If employees are hired or discharged during the year, an adjustment to include only the period of time these employees worked should also be made. If a new employee is hired on October 1 of a calendar-year business, that person worked 3 out of a total of 12 months during the year and is counted as 25 percent, or one-quarter, of a full-time employee.

Although conventional wisdom may indicate that the sales-per-employee ratio should increase every year, in some cases the business's position in its product development cycle can cause this improvement to stall. It is common for IT firms to experience significant fluctuations in development expenditures as products become mature and new ones are developed. The company's sales cycle may run counter to its development initiatives. If the business is at a peak in its product development cycle and at a trough in its revenue cycle, the sales-per-employee figure could be lower—sometimes significantly lower—than its two- to-three-year moving average.

Personnel Cost Ratio

$$\text{Personnel Cost Ratio} = \frac{\text{Personnel Costs}}{\text{Adjusted Net Revenues}}$$

Personnel costs are typically the largest category of expenditures for IT firms. In addition to monitoring the sales per employee, a business should regularly review the ratio of its personnel costs to its adjusted net revenues. In absolute terms, the business's profitability grows as this ratio declines. The ratio indicates how much of every dollar of net adjusted revenues that the business is generating is spent on personnel.

Among the items this metric will reveal is whether the business is increasing its overhead or fixed-cost burden.

Personnel Productivity Ratio

$$\text{Personnel Productivity Ratio} = \frac{\text{Adjusted Net Revenues}}{\text{Personnel Costs}}$$

Another measure that should be monitored is the amount of the adjusted net revenues generated by each dollar expended on personnel costs.

The personnel productivity ratio is the reciprocal or inverse of the personnel cost ratio, with the numerator being adjusted net revenues and the denominator being personnel costs. The business becomes more profitable as this ratio increases, all other facts being unchanged. This ratio indicates the level of adjusted net revenues the business generates for every dollar spent on personnel. It can be used to monitor the same data as the personnel cost ratio.

Hardware Revenue Ratio

$$\text{Hardware Revenue Ratio} = \frac{\text{Net Hardware Sales}}{\text{Adjusted Net Revenues}}$$

Historically, hardware prices have experienced tremendous volatility with a general downward trend. (A variation of Moore's Law thrives outside of the world of microprocessor chips!) The hardware revenue ratio highlights the portion of the business's adjusted net revenues derived from gross margin on hardware. However, if a business resells hardware, for ease of comparison the net hardware sales (that is, gross sales less the cost of the hardware) should be used. This metric minimizes the effect of changing gross hardware prices on the business's overall performance. It monitors the gross margin of hardware plus sales of services and support. This is a more meaningful metric than the gross sales.

A similar calculation should be performed for any category, group or individual item, such as software or services that the business purchases and resells. It is important to carefully monitor these ratios as they relate to items that represent significant revenue components of the business.

Third-Party Revenue Ratio

$$\text{Third-Party Revenue Ratio} = \frac{\text{Adjusted Net Revenues from the Sale of Third-Party Solutions}}{\text{Adjusted Net Revenues}}$$

This ratio highlights the components of a business's revenues that are generated from the sale of products and services that are produced by third parties. It highlights the business's dependence in its suppliers.

If your business resells another business's offerings or solutions, it is subject to risks that are outside its control. Your supplier can introduce highly sought after new offerings, allow its solutions to become obsolete, limit the territory in which the your business can sell its solutions, allow others to encroach on your territory or market, and otherwise change the terms of its agreement with its you or the desirability and demand for its offerings. All of this can have a profound effect on your business's revenues, margins, profits, and cash flow.

Client Revenue Ratios

$$\text{Existing-Client Revenue Ratio} = \frac{\text{Adjusted Net Revenues from Existing Clients}}{\text{Adjusted Net Revenues}}$$

$$\text{New-Client Revenue Ratio} = \frac{\text{Adjusted Net Revenues from New Clients}}{\text{Adjusted Net Revenues}}$$

The existing-client sales ratio should be monitored continually. It highlights the percentage of the firm's net adjusted revenues that will be derived from existing clients, ignoring sales to new customers. As the firm's customer base grows, this metric should rise.

Projections, forecasts, and estimates of revenues from existing clients are an important factor that can be used when evaluating a business's performance. Typically, sales from existing clients can be predicted more easily than ones from new clients. This is true because after a relationship has been formed, the client may regularly share and/or discuss plans for capital expenditures, and you can more easily anticipate the client's buying patterns. Moreover, the same level of advertising, marketing, and promotional expenditures is not required to generate the sale for existing clients as with a new client. Finally, sales from an existing client indicate that the client is satisfied with the company's level of service, which typically bodes well for your business's long-term viability. (It may also indicate you can utilize that client as a reference for potential new clients.)

Even though sales from new clients are more difficult to predict than those from existing clients, they have the ability to increase a business's overall growth significantly. Indeed, depending on the underlying business model, these sales are a vital and sustaining component. New-client sales require time and energy yet can propel your business into new areas, whether in size, volume, type of customer, or industry segment. Moreover, new clients are the basis for future revenue and income streams as they themselves grow and make additional purchases.

Buyers and sellers alike should monitor the new-client sales ratio carefully because it highlights the firm's net adjusted revenues from new clients and illustrates how you have converted new opportunities into revenues.

Maintenance Revenues Ratio

$$\text{Maintenance Revenues Ratio} = \frac{\begin{array}{c}\text{Adjusted Net Revenues}\\\text{from Maintenance}\end{array}}{\text{Adjusted Net Revenues}}$$

It is usual today for IT firms to charge clients for maintenance or postcontract support. For most IT companies, this is an important component of their business model. Some IT companies require that all of their clients purchase extended support in one form or other. This requirement can be contractual or, if not, it can be practical. In the latter situation, the program or application is designed to require annual updates in order to work optimally. A calendar in the software may require yearly reregistration for ongoing compliance with changing laws. One example is the updates for payroll tax filings that must be supplied annually to enable clients to withhold pay and file the appropriate payroll taxes and tax returns.

As a firm's client base grows, the revenues from this segment should increase. Maintenance revenues are particularly enticing to an acquirer because they are easier to predict than other revenue components and, if properly designed, are potentially very profitable. Moreover, if the clients are likely to remain with the IT firm, it generates a fairly predictable future revenue stream.

If it is not already doing so, your company should consider where and whether all of these fees can be increased annually, absolutely, or by percentage; in the latter case, compounding begins to add additional value.

QUICK TIP

An owner of a software business should not lose sight of the value of compounding. One simple example illustrates this. If you were given the choice of accepting either (a) a million dollars or (b) one cent per day, which is doubled daily for 30 days, which would you choose? Initially many would say they would choose $1 million; however, the payout that begins with one cent on the first day of the month ends with a payout of $5,368,709.12 on the thirtieth day, resulting in a total payout for all 30 days of $10,737,418.23.

The selling price of your business increases when the perceived risks of operating it are reduced, and when a buyer can reasonably predict revenues, the acquisition is much more attractive. Predictable revenues allow management the luxury of creating budgets with the security that they will have the cash flow to fund company needs for human resources, capital expenditures, and physical expansion. All technology firms, for sale or not, should give regular and serious consideration to the structure and pricing of maintenance, support, and upgrade fees.

Software Revenues Ratio

$$\text{Software Revenues Ratio} = \frac{\text{Adjusted Net Revenues from Software}}{\text{Adjusted Net Revenues}}$$

For many IT firms, revenues from internally developed software products are extremely profitable once the research and development costs have been recovered. Software revenues can have higher gross-margin percentages than other sources of revenue. However, much software has a limited life, quickly becoming obsolete. As a result, it is incumbent on IT firms to continually update and develop new software solutions and upgrade existing ones to the extent to which they are effectively new ones. This process should be a part of every IT business, even those in the midst of being sold, not to mention any whose owners are contemplating a sale in the future. The continued pipeline of "new and improved" products will bolster a firm's value and provide a real hedge in the event the sale is not consummated. An internally developed software application is the most valuable to your company, as well as to a potential buyer, when it is just being introduced to the market and receiving wide acceptance and acclaim.

However, because the development cycle for software frequently stretches beyond one calendar or fiscal year, this may be another ratio that should be averaged, possibly on a weighted basis, over several years.

Service Revenues Ratio

$$\text{Service Revenues Ratio} = \frac{\text{Adjusted Net Revenues from Services}}{\text{Adjusted Net Revenues}}$$

Service revenues (which are distinct from maintenance, support, and upgrade fees) are another vital component of most IT business sales. The unpredictability of increases in labor costs results in gross margins varying widely. In certain instances, companies have been able to compensate for increased labor costs by raising service fees. But for competitive and other business reasons, this may not always be possible. Regardless, your company's services revenues always should be closely examined to determine both current profitability and any potential for future increases.

QUICK TIP

A business that permits its support fees to remain stagnant is accepting, or acquiescing, to a real (or inflation adjusted) decline in fees.

When generating service revenues, your business's employees interact with customers, creating an opportunity to monitor and improve existing relationships, market additional services or products, and assess new opportunities.

QUICK TIP

Your business should consider (if it has not already done so) designing incentives to encourage all employees who interact with customers even if they are not in a direct sales function to be alert to opportunities that can generate additional sales.

Large-Client Dependency Ratio

$$\text{Large-Client Dependency Ratio} = \frac{\text{Adjusted Net Revenues from Largest Clients}}{\text{Adjusted Net Revenues}}$$

The acquirer of a business assumes more risk if one client or a handful of clients generates a significant portion of your revenues. The loss (or potential loss) of a large client will have a profound impact on the business and its sale value. However, it is common for an IT firm, whether it operates in a few vertical markets or across different markets horizontally, to have contracts with a few large clients or key channels in a year in which a product is installed or a major upgrade is performed. If the particular clients rotate or change from year to year, this risk is mitigated as compared with a business that continues to rely on the same few key accounts every year. But even under these circumstances, a company will have an ongoing need to obtain the customers necessary to sustain and grow the business. The large-client dependency ratio calculates the percentage of the revenues generated by a business's largest clients.

When calculating the ratio, the gross profit generated by each large client should be calculated and analyzed continually. It is important for both seller and buyer to be circumspect about this metric, as large customers frequently negotiate significant price reductions, require (or at least receive) a high level of service (reducing margins from their sales), and are often enough delinquent when paying their bills. These attributes can cause operating expenses to rise and margins to fall.

In some situations, the loss of large clients will not have a significant effect on the business's bottom line, although it will decrease top-line growth. You should analyze your large accounts continually to ascertain their overall profitability.

Monthly Sustenance Ratio

$$\text{Monthly Sustenance Ratio} = \frac{\text{Monthly Sustenance Level (MSL)}}{\text{Monthly Adjusted Net Revenues}}$$

The monthly sustenance ratio calculates the percentage of your company's adjusted net revenues as compared to its fixed costs. This is a modified fixed-cost ratio. Reducing this ratio minimizes the overall operational risk and enables your company to take advantage of opportunities, because less of its revenues are being absorbed by fixed costs.

The cost of personnel is the largest expense for most IT companies. Therefore, serious consideration should be given to instituting incentive-based compensation plans, in which the fixed, or base, component of compensation is reduced for as many employees (at an appropriate level) as is feasible. The implementation of an incentive-based compensation plan can reduce a company's sustenance ratio. It will also eliminate automatic or "institutionalized" companywide increases, which can impede innovation, when business is stagnant overall. Conversely, when the business does well, the compensation paid to the responsible employees should rise.

$$\text{Discretionary Payroll Ratio} = \frac{\text{Incentive-Based Personnel Costs}}{\text{Personnel Costs Exclusive of Incentive-Based Compensation}}$$

The discretionary payroll ratio is a supplement to the monthly sustenance ratio. It calculates the portion of your business's payroll costs that are incentive-based compared with the non–incentive-based or fixed payroll costs. This author feels that to motivate employees properly, there should be an incentive-based component in every employee's compensation package. Typically this component's share of total compensation should increase with the employee's responsibility.

The adoption of a properly designed incentive-based compensation plan provides several competitive advantages to management. It more tightly aligns employees' goals with those of the business, and it reduces the business's cash needs during its less robust periods. The higher the discretionary payroll ratio, the less reserves the company must maintain during slow times.

QUICK TIP

Typically it is not practical to reduce an employee's base salary, as a result, a significant portion of the future increases should be incentive-based.

MSL Coverage Ratios

$$\text{Fast MSL Coverage} = \frac{\text{Cash}}{\text{Monthly Sustenance Level}}$$

The fast MSL coverage ratio calculates the percentage or multiple of a company's monthly sustenance level that can be paid with its current cash balance. This indicates the level of cash reserves your company has on hand to pay its anticipated monthly expenses. It is one measure of your business's current financial strength.

$$\text{MSL Coverage} = \frac{\text{Cash} + \text{Accounts Receivable to Be Collected in 30 Days}}{\text{Monthly Sustenance Level}}$$

This measure, which is similar to the fast MSL coverage ratio, compares your company's cash plus the receivables expected to be collected within 30 days with the business's monthly sustenance level. This ratio is helpful if the collection of receivables is reasonably predictable. If it is common to collect all or almost all or your firm's accounts receivable within a period other than 30 days, that time period can be utilized when calculating this metric.

Prepaid Cash and Liquidity

$$\text{Prepaid Cash} = \text{Cash} - \text{Client Deposits (Prepayments)}$$

The prepaid-cash figure represents the portion of an IT company's cash that is being provided by its customers in the form of deposits, prepayments, or deferred revenues. It calculates the portion of the cash for which your company has yet to perform services. If this metric is negative, it indicates that if your company were to liquidate, it would not have sufficient cash to repay clients for prepaid services or services not yet performed. As clients typically will prepay their fees only if (1) they desire additional goods and services and (2) are confident that the business will perform its duties. This metric helps measure client satisfaction.

For purposes of the prepaid cash calculation (as well as the prepaid liquidity calculation that follows), client deposits include all prepayments made by customers for services not yet performed or products not yet delivered. In certain instances these are referred to as prepaid revenues or deferred revenues on your business's balance sheet.

QUICK TIP

Every business should explore the possibility of having its clients finance a portion of its operations. Unless the business needs to offer substantial discounts to obtain these funds, this alternative may be less expensive than turning to banks, which is the traditional route of financing, or factoring receivables.

$$\text{Prepaid Liquidity} = \text{Cash} + \text{Accounts Receivable} - \text{Client Deposits (Prepayments or Unearned Revenues)}$$

The prepaid liquidity figure is similar to the prepaid cash calculation but is expanded to include the portion of the business's cash, plus accounts receivable, that are not funded by client deposits. As is the case with prepaid cash, this figure indicates the portion of your most liquid assets that are *not* being funded by customers. This figure will be more meaningful if all uncollectible receivables are deducted from the calculation and the time period when the receivables will be collected can be reasonably predicted.

Employee Utilization

$$\text{Employee Utilization (hours)} = \frac{\text{Hours Billed}}{\text{Hours Worked}}$$

$$\text{Employee Utilization (dollars)} = \frac{\text{Revenues Generated}}{\text{Employee's Compensation}}$$

Whenever an IT business is billing for its employees' time, which typically take the form of "professional", "client", or "consulting" services, it should monitor the utilization of the individuals (as well as the entire group) on an ongoing basis. Many businesses have seasonal fluctuations that can result in variations of these rates throughout the year. Moreover, new employees typically require more training and education and have lower utilization rates until they become more familiar with the systems, clients, and procedures. Most new employees cannot be billable much of the time, much less all of it. Even the most billable and seasoned employees need downtime, unrelated to client matters, to perform administrative tasks, learn new skills, and interact with other individuals at the company. Each business should set an overall target utilization rate for their employees who bill based on their time.

In addition, although individuals can and do frequently work more than a 40-hour week, typically there are limits to how much anyone can continue to work effectively at such a rate. However, there are always exceptions to this. Notwithstanding these exceptions, there are limits to the ability of your employees to increase their ratios to desired levels in a given year after experiencing several slow months in which they were not fully utilized. The hours billed should be compared with the hours worked (both group and individual), and a similar ratio that is dollar-based should be calculated to compare the revenue the individual generates with his or her compensation.

Administrative Employee Cost Ratio

$$\text{Administrative Employee Cost Ratio} = \frac{\text{Administrative Personnel Costs}}{\text{Total Personnel Costs}}$$

Your company should monitor what portion of total personnel costs are for administrative personnel. It is common for growing as well as established companies to become bloated with administrative personnel, which of course reduces profits and possibly stifles growth. This ratio should be reviewed and analyzed (by both sellers and buyers) in tandem with the sales-per-employee figure, personnel cost or personnel productivity ratios, and the business's overall profitability. This ratio should be adjusted to reflect any administrative functions that are outsourced.

Client Acquisition Costs

$$\text{Client Acquisition Cost Ratio} = \frac{\text{Costs of Obtaining New Clients}}{\text{Gross Margin}}$$

Your business should constantly monitor the costs of obtaining new customers or clients.

One method that has been developed to gauge the effectiveness and efficiency of obtaining new clients is the client acquisition cost ratio. This ratio compares the costs of obtaining new clients with the gross margin.

Over time, this ratio should decline as the gross margin grows faster than the client acquisition costs.

If a business does not segregate its marketing and sales costs for new versus established clients, a reasonable estimate should be used. It is this author's experience that the costs of new clients can be three quarters or more of a business's total marketing and sales expenses. However, since this figure is specific to a given business, an analysis or informed approximation should be undertaken.

If this ratio fails to decline for a particular business that is not entering a new market, it may be a harbinger of a broken or invalid business model or poor market acceptance, all of which do not bode well for the long-term viability of the entity.

INTERNAL MANAGEMENT REPORTS

In addition to the metrics just discussed, every business should also prepare the following reports on a monthly or bimonthly basis:

Cash Flow Projection for the Next 12 to 24 Months

Every business should maintain a cash flow projection for one or two years. The cash flow projection is different from a profit-and-loss projection since it analyzes the cash that will be received and expended by your business. Although your sales may be very high in a particular period, a lag between closing the sale and the anticipated, let alone the actual, collection date can have a severe impact on the business. This impact will be even more serious if the business experiences an unexpected delay in collection. Every business should monitor its cash flow continually.

QUICK TIP

Cash flow projections should add back noncash expenditures, such as depreciation and amortization. They should also deduct any other uses of cash that are not reflected as operating expenses, such as capital expenditures.

Work Backlog (Covering the Next 12 to 18 Months)

Every business should always maintain a listing of the orders of all types (software, hardware, services) that it has received but not yet fulfilled. This listing, which should include revenues to be received as well as person-days that need to be expended to generate those revenues, is a valuable tool for managing your business. It clearly will assist in determining staffing needs and cash flow requirements. This schedule also decreases the risk that a buyer assumes in the purchase, because it represents work that will need to be performed in the immediate future.

Sales Prospects or Pipeline

Every business should maintain a list of sales prospects, imminent or not, as well as a sales pipeline indicating the likelihood of various prospects becoming actual sales over the next 6, 12 and 18 months. As your business's offerings become more complex, the time from contact to contract generally becomes longer. Although the sales department should provide input, in most cases salespeople are overly optimistic, so the listing should be based on objective, discernible standards (see Exhibit 6.1) that are reviewed by management before they are included in the list.

Each prospect's gross sales, and possibly even gross margin, should be multiplied by a factor to determine the likelihood of its recurrence, and the resulting figure should be used in the sales prospect list. The likelihood factor should be conservative, to allow for unanticipated problems, and be based on objective standards reviewed by both the sales manager and a nonsales executive before finalization. Some examples of hypothetical objective factors and possible conservative probabilities for sales pipeline are shown in Exhibit 6.1.

Exhibit 6.1 merely shows examples for illustrative purposes. Each company should develop its own criteria for objectively analyzing prospective sales.

EXHIBIT 6.1   EVENTS AND LIKELIHOOD OF SALE— HYPOTHETICAL

Event	Likelihood of Sale
a. Customer makes follow-up request after receiving initial information.	5%
b. Salesperson determines if customer has budgeted sufficient funds for purchase.	10%
c. Prospective customer indicates a high level of interest in the offering, such as requesting on-site demonstration, making reference calls to other customers, etc.	33%
d. Customer indicates very high interest in offerings, such as requesting formal proposal and scheduling the time for determination by purchasing committee.	66%
e. Purchasing committee approves purchase (details of contract need to be resolved) and submits it to board of directors.	75%
f. Company signs contract and indicates commitment to go forward with project.	95%

Financial Forecast and Projection

Every IT business should prepare a one- to two-year forecast and projection every year. The process of preparing and compiling these data will assist your business and its managers in planning for future needs in personnel, IT systems, physical facilities, and marketing and working capital requirements.

Year-to-Date Financial Statements

One of the best tools to monitor overall performance is the business's year-to-date financial statements. It is of paramount importance that this document be prepared and distributed within a few days after every month-end, as the utility of the year-to-date financial statements as an ongoing management tool decreases rapidly over time.

All of this information, as well as whatever other data you feel are necessary to gauge the performance of your business, should be distributed in a regular and timely manner to your managers. You should consider sharing certain key metrics with all employees at companywide meetings. It is important to explain how the metrics are calculated and their significance to the business. If properly explained and not cumbersome or irrelevant, these metrics can become motivational and can also enable the business's employees in their decision making.

CHAPTER 7

Your Board

In this post–dot-com bubble, post-Enron period, the importance of an active, independent board takes on even greater importance. Concomitantly, the responsibilities and potential liability of board members have mushroomed.

In most jurisdictions, a business's certificate of incorporation or bylaws provide for a board of directors. If your business operates as a limited liability company (LLC), there is typically a certificate of formation instead. Moreover, an LLC has managers instead of a board of directors. For ease of discussion, this chapter will refer to a corporation, but similar advice pertains, and similar actions can be performed, for an LLC, partnership, or other legal entities.

Exhibit 7.1 lists the terms utilized by corporations, limited liability companies, and a third type, partnerships.

EXHIBIT 7.1 **TERMS USED BY CORPORATIONS, LLCS, AND PARTNERSHIPS**

Corporation	LLC	Partnership
Stock	Membership interest	Partnership interest
Shareholder	Member	Partner
Dividend	Distribution	Drawing
Board of directors	Managers	Managing partners
Bylaws and Shareholders agreement	Operating agreement	Partnership agreement
Certificate of incorporation	Certificate of formation	Partnership agreement (A certificate may need to be filed with the state or county.)

BRINGING OUTSIDERS IN

Optimally, the board should have a majority of its members who are outsiders. Only one or two insiders—usually the business's chief executive officer and one other key employee, such as the chief operating officer, chief financial officer, or chief technology officer—should be included. The suggested or preferred total is three or five members: one or two insiders and two or three outsiders. Frequently it is preferable for the board to consist of an odd number of people to avoid any tie votes.

Some business owners have found it more constructive to build their boards slowly, by electing only one outsider initially. This method elongates the process of building a board, as everyone's comfort level increases and the benefits of the board become more apparent. It is this author's belief that smaller boards allow for faster decisions but concentrate more power with insiders, and a smaller board also can limit the range of available ideas, skills, resources, and contacts. A well-constructed, diversified board of five members can yield far greater benefits to your business than one that is smaller, especially when it is also homogenous. The synergy of the outside and inside directors can provide a unique prospective to the business.

Using their individual and combined talents and expertise, the board of directors should provide guidance on the company's overall strategy. This guidance includes setting objectives and advising and challenging management to achieve them. For the board to be effective, the members must be granted full and unfettered access to all aspects of the business and its operations.

Serving on the board should be a long-term commitment. To attract and retain qualified outsiders, you as owner probably will have to give up some control. Within their areas of expertise, some outsiders may be far more knowledgeable than you, which can be very helpful to your business. If you and your colleagues choose and utilize the board wisely, the enterprise can evolve and grow to levels that it has not previously achieved. Naturally your business then becomes much more valuable and attractive to buyers of all types, including potential investors, venture capitalists, and private equity funds.

Sarbanes-Oxley

As a result of the enactment of the Sarbanes-Oxley Act (SOX), the fiduciary duty of the directors and officers assumes even greater importance. This is especially true if your business will be sold to a publicly held business, in which the buyer's chief executive officer and chief financial officer will have to certify to the accuracy of the business's financial statements and internal controls, including the results of the acquired businesses.

SOX also contains provisions that criminalize document destruction, alteration, and concealment along with retaliatory acts against employee whistle-blowers.

In the past, motto was "Buyer beware." However, with the enactment of SOX, the seller also needs to beware and to understand how SOX may impact the sale of a privately held company.

Directors' and Officers' Insurance

Before an outsider is elected to the board of directors, it is usually of paramount importance to the outsider that your business have directors' and officers' insurance in place. Although the premiums may seem high, it is money well spent. It will encourage and enable qualified people to serve on your business's board of directors. In today's litigious business environment, even the costs of defending a frivolous lawsuit can be staggering. One way to minimize the cost of this insurance is to purchase an insurance policy with a high deductible. This will provide protection against large expenditures but require your business to pay a predetermined amount on any claim. But this protection from the business can evaporate if it files for bankruptcy. An outside director typically will request that your company adopt a resolution indemnifying the directors for any expenses they incur defending themselves in any lawsuits as a result of their position.

Ground Rules

Business owners should consider carefully whom they would like to serve as their board members. For example, your firm's Certified Public Accountants (CPAs) should not be placed on the board. Doing so would eliminate his or her independent status, and he or she could not serve as your business's outside auditors without a substantial disclaimer. Such disclosure would limit the utility of the financial statements that the CPA or the CPA's firm prepares.

You and the board members must have mutual and reciprocated trust and confidence. The board will be discussing and advising on sensitive issues, such as ownership structure, exit strategies, human resources, compensation, strategic planning, mergers, acquisitions, competition, sales, financing, and new ventures. Without a high level of trust, the relationship between you and the board will not be productive. This is not to say that everyone on the board should always agree and not question others' ideas. A board must not consist of sycophants.

All boards, regardless of size and composition, need tools, forums, and resources to assist their businesses. For example, agendas should be circulated in advance of meetings, and minutes should be prepared and distributed shortly after every meeting's conclusion. Distributing a preliminary agenda in advance of the meeting encourages everyone to focus on the items that need to be addressed and allows board members to prepare adequately. Receiving the minutes shortly afterward reminds members of what was covered and can serve as a checklist of action items. More important, it permits a review, afterward in isolation, of items that were agreed to, including ones that may have been agreed to too hastily, and it highlights potential dilemmas, concerns, conflicts, or issues that may arise down the road that during the meeting itself may have been skated over or otherwise inadequately addressed.

This author believes a business's board of directors should meet every four to eight weeks, every two months at the least, although more frequent meetings may be appropriate if your firm is growing rapidly or as new, complex issues emerge. To increase both attendance and productivity, meetings should be scheduled well in advance and rarely canceled. Board members should make a commitment to attend all meetings. Telephone and video conferences should be used to address emergent issues that arise between meetings.

Your company should consider setting up a secure Web site to house agendas, minutes, contact information, and other resources, as well as intraboard e-mail. During meetings, all board members must commit to minimizing outside distractions, such as use of cell phones, PDAs, or Blackberries/Treos.

Compensation for board members is a key but vexing issue. To attract top-quality people, your business should be prepared to offer a reasonable rate for the individuals' time, as well as options to purchase equity or some other equity-sharing component. If your business is willing and able to pay for travel expenses, this will expand the geographic area from which members can be chosen, which may significantly improve the board's diversity and value to the business. Although many businesses pay their directors by the meeting, it may be more prudent to compensate them annually, or in some hybrid combination of the two. In today's fast-paced world, your business may not be able to wait to receive board advice until a meeting is convened, and paying members yearly or partly so sends a message that a director's work is ongoing and may need to be performed before, after, and during meetings.

In the long run, though, it makes the most sense for you to provide some equity or equity-sharing component that minimizes the business's short-term cash requirements while aligning the directors' goals with those of your company.

CHAPTER 8

Marketing Your Business for Sale

Once you have prepared your information technology business for sale, the next step is to market it discreetly but effectively to potential buyers. This process often can make or break a sale. Developing a plan to inform potential buyers that your business is available must balance the need to draw the interest of a number of different parties while still maintaining confidentiality. Also, at this point it may make sense for your company to engage the services of an intermediary such as professional business advisor, investment banker, or broker who can seek out and interact with potential acquirers while you concentrate on running the business. (You and your staff probably should be prepared, both emotionally and tactically, for word to be inadvertently disseminated regardless of the precautions you may take.)

BUSINESS OVERVIEW

The first step in marketing your IT business is to prepare a brief description and overview of the business. Your selling memorandum, "memo," or "book" will form the basis for this description. However, the description must be reviewed carefully by your advisors to ensure not only that it is up-to-date and accurate but also that it is easy to understand and includes the appropriate disclaimers. This document should be encompassing but concise. Utilizing business plans as the basis for the book or selling memorandum were discussed in Chapter 4.

This chapter identifies some of the key areas typically covered in the "book" or selling memorandum and an engagement letter with an intermediary.

Frequently the cover page of the "book" or "memo" contains a notice, in boldface, along these lines:

- The information is being released pursuant to a signed confidentiality agreement.
- The information should be kept confidential.
- The information, including projections and forecasts, may not be accurate.
- The buyer should conduct his or her own due diligence before entering into any transaction.
- The seller is under no obligation to continue negotiations with the recipient.
- The names of individuals with whom the seller should limit their communication about the proposed transaction.

Exhibit 8.1 contains an example of a sample disclaimer.

The next step is compiling and contacting a list of potential buyers. Keep in mind that this can be a double-edged sword: The more people who are contacted about your business being for sale, the greater the likelihood that a buyer will be found, and the greater the risk that someone will reveal (inadvertently or not) that the business is for sale.

Typically, the people most likely to purchase your business are also those whom you do not want to have confidential information about your operations. Included in this group are your customers, suppliers, and competitors. As a result, you must gauge the interest, sincerity, and integrity of each potential contact carefully. If you or one of your advisors has a business or personal relationship or knows someone who has a business or personal relationship with any of them, that relationship can move the process along and possibly allay your fears. Certainly, competitors who have previously expressed any interest in purchasing your business should be approached—discreetly. It may be preferable to meet or speak with contacts to determine if you want to discuss a possible transaction with them before exchanging any substantive information.

EXHIBIT 8.1 SAMPLE DISCLAIMER

Terms and Conditions of Submission and Receipt

This Selling Memorandum ("the Memorandum") has been prepared by The Chalfin Group Inc. ("TCGI") solely for informational purposes from information supplied by Selling Company Inc. ("Sellco" or "the Company"). TCGI is furnishing this Memorandum as the authorized agent for Sellco solely for use by prospective purchasers when evaluating whether to acquire the Company. By accepting the Memorandum, the recipient acknowledges and agrees that it is being submitted pursuant to an executed confidentiality agreement.

The information in this Memorandum is not all-inclusive and does not contain all of the information that a prospective purchaser may desire. Any interested party should conduct its own independent investigation and analysis of the Company.

This Memorandum includes certain statements, estimates, and projections provided by Sellco with respect to the anticipated future performance of the Company. TCGI has not independently verified any of the information contained herein, including the assumptions on which the projections, estimates, and forecasts are based. Neither TCGI nor Sellco or any of their employees, agents, or affiliates make any representations or warranties as to the accuracy or completeness of the information contained in the Memorandum or any other oral, written, or other communication transmitted to the recipient in the course of its evaluation of the Company. The only representations and warranties that will be made will be contained in a definitive agreement relating to the sale of the Company that will be executed by both the purchaser and Sellco.

The Company and TCGI reserve the right to simultaneously negotiate with more than one prospective purchaser and may enter into a definitive sale agreement without prior notice to the recipient or other potential purchasers. The Company reserves the right to terminate its participation in the sale process or to modify its procedures without prior notice or without providing a reason. Any agreement for the sale of the Company will be in the form of a written definitive agreement executed by both the Company and the purchaser.

Potential purchasers should keep their involvement in this process confidential. They should not communicate with Company, its personnel, or affiliates unless they receive prior written approval from TCGI.

Any questions or communications relating to the Memorandum and the proposed transaction should be referred to:

Robert J. Chalfin, President
The Chalfin Group Inc.
45 Bridge Street; P.O. Box 4519
Metuchen, New Jersey 08840-4519

Telephone 732/321-1099
Facsimile 732/321-1066
bob@chalfin.com

However, most of your competitors, suppliers, and customers can and probably already have information on your business, including your key customers, offerings, and revenues.

Chapter 3 discusses the types of buyers. However, regardless of the range of buyer motives, the price paid for a business usually rises if a potential acquirer knows others are interested in bidding. Oftentimes more than one interested acquirer will emerge. In general, if a business is being sought by a strategic suitor or if there is more than one potential buyer, the key is to contact these entities as quickly as possible to generate increased interest in the business and to maximize the sale price.

Creating an auction, whether it is formal or informal, typically will benefit the seller. You stand a much greater chance of increasing your price and entering into a more lucrative transaction if the potential suitors know they are competing with others who have sufficient resources to consummate the deal.

The auction can be a formal one, in which each participant knows the identity of the other and there are strict rules regarding deadlines for submission acceptance and rejection of offers and counteroffers, the form of offers, and required terms; or it can be an informal process, but one in which there are several bidders.

The mere suggestion that you will conduct an auction for the company may cause a highly motivated purchaser to avoid this process by making a preemptive bid. Assuming you, as the seller, are comfortable with the offer, accepting it will avoid the dissemination of your business's data to numerous potential buyers and may expedite the sale process.

Although you do not have to let potential suitors know each other's identity, astute participants will be able to determine most of the other likely participants.

Keep in mind that *premature* disclosure of a possible sale to employees, customers, suppliers, or competitors can be very harmful. Employees, customers, and suppliers alike may feel insecure about being involved with a business that is in the process of being sold. The mere rumor of a sale may cause key employees and customers to leave. And competitors may broadcast these rumors and use them to lure prospective or existing customers, pirate your employees, and otherwise damage your business's reputation.

WAYS TO MARKET YOUR BUSINESS

There are a variety of ways to get the word out that you are ready to sell. You may contact potential buyers via letter; indeed, you may advertise your business through newspapers or trade journals, or on the Internet. But it is preferable to be discreet and use an intermediary, such as an investment banker/business broker or consultant who is familiar with the IT industry and understands the importance of confidentiality.

Using an Intermediary

Retaining the services of an intermediary such as a professional business advisor or broker to market your business can be a wise move. The intermediary's fee often proves to be a good investment, particularly if the intermediary puts you in touch with a bona fide buyer, negotiates a better price than you could have on your own, saves you a significant amount of time and aggravation during the process, and/or expedites the sale, enabling it to occur sooner than otherwise.

Engaging the services of an intermediary allows you to devote your time to what you do best—operating the business. Selling any business can easily become a full-time job, and owners who neglect the business while selling it hurt their own cause. It is very common for a business to suffer a decline during the year of an actual, delayed, or failed sale, because key personnel cannot concentrate fully on operations. This will make the business less desirable to subsequent suitors. As it is common for negotiations with a potential buyer to terminate for a variety of reasons throughout the process, this possibility should not be ignored. The intermediary can also screen potential buyers and help you avoid expending precious time with ones who do not meet your criteria or do not have the financial, management, and other resources to consummate the transaction.

> **QUICK TIP**
>
> A good business intermediary has knowledge of the market and is aware of the prices being paid for companies comparable to yours. This individual can assess the specific elements that improve or detract from the value of your business.

Using a qualified intermediary also ensures that the deal will be handled on a professional, rather than personal, level. The sale of a business can become a surprisingly emotional event, particularly if negotiations are protracted and/or difficult, and it can be extremely helpful to have an experienced professional on your team assisting as you make decisions and accompanying you through the process, while at the same time buffering you from aspects of the negotiations that can impinge on the buyer's relationship with you and your key employees after the sale is consummated.

You should consider the type, scope, and extent of services that you will require. For example, you may merely want your business listed on various databases to gain a wide range of exposure to potential buyers. Conversely, you may only want a small select group of potential buyers to be informed, on a confidential basis, by your advisor that your business is for sale. You may want your advisor to have a very limited role or to manage and oversee the entire process, from the initial planning through the ultimate consummation of the sale.

Engaging the services of an intermediary also removes a potential roadblock from the sale process: you. Many successful businesspeople have difficulty disengaging. A second problem, in addition to the sale becoming too personal, might be that your presence may showcase your value as the owner. If buyers perceive that the business cannot continue effectively without you, typically it will decrease the price and/or result in the sale entailing a long-term employment commitment by you.

Your advisors should also be able to provide you with guidance concerning the crafting and design of a transaction, as well as counseling when you should accept or reject an offer.

Finally, experienced business advisors may be better negotiators than you are. They are not likely to be intimidated by potential buyers. They offer a different perspective, and they understand where compromises should and should not be made. Furthermore, they have experience in keeping negotiations afloat during difficult times and may be able to see a complicated or seemingly failing deal through to the end.

While every engagement contains its own nuances which should be reflected in the terms of the retention of the intermediary, a sample engagement letter or contract with a business intermediary, whether it is a business broker, investment banker, or consultant, frequently covers these items:

- Who determines asking price
- Who prepares the selling memo book
- Period of engagement
- Compensation to intermediary
- Termination procedure
- "Tag-along" rights
- Basis for fee
- Payment terms
- Contingent payments
- Deposits/retainer
- Expense reimbursement

See Exhibit 8.2 for a sample intermediary agreement, which assumes that the parties have already signed a Confidentiality Agreement.

Remuneration of Intermediaries/Business Broker/Investment Bankers

Intermediaries/business brokers/investment bankers typically charge a fee based on the sale price of the business. The fee is usually a percentage of the total price; however, it can follow a number of different formulas.

Some traditional formulas provide for a regressive commission rate in which the broker receives a lower rate for each marginal dollar of sale price that is obtained. Many observers, including this author, believe there is some merit to structuring the fee so it is progressive, and the commission rate increases with the sales price. For example, the success fee could be one rate on a predetermined amount of the sale price and a higher rate on any portion of the sale price that exceeds the predetermined amount.

The reasoning behind this is to provide the intermediary with an incentive to obtain the highest possible sale price for the seller. If the intermediary is compensated under a formula in which the rate declines as the sale price increases, there is little monetary incentive for him or her to negotiate a higher sales price when the offer is at a given level. Ultimately this may be disadvantageous to the seller.

EXHIBIT 8.2   SAMPLE INTERMEDIARY AGREEMENT

Date

Mr./Ms. President

Dear......:

You have requested that The Chalfin Group Inc. ("TCGI") assist with the sale of your business.

To streamline the process and avoid time and billing charges, I propose that we have a monthly retainer of $____ plus disbursements (Retainer). Sellco would also be responsible for reimbursing TCGI for any travel and any other out-of-pocket expenses.

In connection with the sale of your business, TCGI will perform the following:

a. Prepare, with your help, a selling memorandum,
b. Determine, with your assistance, a reasonable asking price for Sellco,
c. Compile a list of potential purchasers of Sellco,
d. Contact and meet with the potential purchasers of Sellco,
e. Negotiate the sale of Sellco,
f. Coordinate the sale of Sellco. This would include preparing for and participating in the due diligence process and coordinating the work of Sellco's attorneys and CPAs.

In addition to the above, Sellco, or its shareholders, will pay TCGI a success fee (Success Fee) of a) __ percent of the total sale price of any stock or assets sold by Sellco or its shareholders outside the ordinary course of business on the first $ ____, plus b) ____percent of the total sale price of any stock or assets sold by Sellco or its shareholders in excess of $___million.

a. The Success Fee shall be based upon the gross sale price and any other economic benefits accruing to the Sellco or its shareholders, including any covenants against competition or consulting in excess of current salary levels. For the purpose of calculating the Success Fee, the consideration shall include the gross amount paid by the Buyer, plus (i) the assumption of or repayment of any indebtedness due to any external financing source or affiliate of the Company and (ii) the value of any assets, net of liabilities, if retained by the company or by the shareholders. The consideration shall not be reduced for any taxes or other costs incurred.

b. If the transaction consummated by the Company or its shareholders includes a "contingent payment," TCGI and Sellco shall mutually attempt to agree on the net present value of such payments. TCGI's Success Fee would then be calculated including the net present value of the future contingent payments. If TCGI and Sellco do not agree on the net present value of the contingent payments, then TCGI shall receive its Success Fees attributable to the contingent payment as such payment occurs.

c. TCGI will be entitled to the Success Fee with regard to any transaction consummated or for which a binding contract has been entered into i) within _____ months of the termination or ii) within ____ months of the termination with any party listed on the schedule of potential buyers as defined in paragraph d, below (or affiliates thereof).

EXHIBIT 8.2   CONTINUED

d. At any time after _____ months from the date of this agreement, either party may terminate this agreement by providing thirty days' written notice to the other party. Upon termination of our services, TCGI will prepare a list of companies ("schedule of potential buyers") that TCGI contacted or were in direct contact with during the initial term.

The Success Fee calculated above shall be paid in full at closing. The portion of the Success Fee attributable to a contingent payment shall be paid at the time the contingent payment is received. The retainer shall be paid at the beginning of each calendar month beginning on _____, and the disbursements shall be paid within 30 days of your receipt of TCGI's invoice.

It is understood that TCGI is being engaged solely to provide consulting services only and that neither TCGI nor any of its principals or employees is being engaged solely to provide legal or accounting advice. No lawyer-client or accountant-client relationship is created as a result of this engagement.

Kindly review this letter, and if you agree, sign below; however, if you have any questions on any part of this letter, please call me immediately. I am hopeful this will be the start of a long and mutually beneficial relationship between our firms.

Very truly yours,

THE CHALFIN GROUP INC.

Robert J. Chalfin

RJC:rs

I have read and agree to the terms and provisions of this letter.

Sellco Inc.

_____

Mr./Ms. Sam Seller   Date
President

It is this author's opinion that the additional marginal commission, although initially appearing more expensive, may be worth the cost if the sale process is expedited, if the owner receives additional net proceeds, and if the transaction is successfully consummated.

The agreements with the broker typically will provide that the seller can terminate the agreement after a period of time, with notice.

Brokers typically request "tag-along rights." These rights typically provide that if the potential seller terminates the agreement with the broker, the broker will still receive the commission if the sale occurs to anyone with whom the broker had contact with over a predetermined time after the termination of the agreement; and the broker may also receive the commission if the sale occurs over a shorter period of time to anyone, regardless whether the broker had contact with that party. This provision prevents sellers from terminating the agreement just prior to the sale. The agreement may also provide that the broker receive a commission if he or she produces a bona fide buyer but the seller ultimately decides not to sell.

Many brokers require that a seller pay a retainer or up-front fee, plus expenses throughout the entire process. The up-front fee may or may not be deducted from the commission in the event that the sale is consummated, but is not refundable if the sale does not occur.

Another issue arises if the sale requires that contingent payment be made in the future. In that case, the broker can either receive his or her commission at the time the seller is paid or both the seller and broker can agree to calculate the present value of such payments and the broker would be paid a percentage of it. The agreement should provide that, if they cannot agree on the present value, the broker would receive a share of the commission on the contingent payments as the seller is paid them.

CHAPTER 9

Valuing Your Business: An Introduction

Before you can sell your information technology business, it is best to know how much it is worth. In other words, you must begin the valuation process. This process can be complex, but if you do it well, you will have a clearer view of the true value of your business and will be able to negotiate with potential buyers with more confidence. Moreover, before you attempt to sell, you must determine your minimum acceptable price, having compared it with the business's fair market value.

This chapter, along with Chapters 10, 11, and 12, offers guidance on valuation, including factors to consider, steps you may be able to take to increase your business's value, and various valuation methods in common use.

Buyers may be willing to pay different prices depending on their motives or needs for wanting your business, as was discussed in Chapter 3.

Although all sellers want to portray their business's best attributes to potential buyers, every one of your claims must be accurate. It is reasonable to assume that buyers are intelligent, well informed, and will diligently verify your representations, so any false or even misleading representations can have ongoing negative repercussions during the deal and afterward.

FAIR MARKET VALUE

The first step in the valuation process is to determine your business's fair market value. Fair market value is defined in Revenue Ruling 59-60 as the price at which property would change hands between a willing buyer and a willing seller when neither is under any compulsion to buy or sell, and both parties have reasonable knowledge of all relevant matters affecting the business. The two components of this definition—the parties' willingness and their information—both merit further attention.

The phrase "willing buyer and willing seller" signifies that neither party is being forced into the transaction. When circumstances create special pressure for either buyer or seller, often the conditions of the sale are affected. For example, if key employees recently have left the business to seek employment with a competitor, or the sale is required immediately as a result of the loss, such as the death or disability, of a shareholder or key employee, the business typically will receive less than its fair market value immediately prior to the event that caused a forced sale. On the other hand, a buyer who feels compelled to purchase a particular business for competitive reasons within a very short time may well find him- or herself willingly paying a price more than its fair market value.

The requirement that both parties have reasonable knowledge of all relevant facts also means that one party does not have superior knowledge. This advantage might be knowledge of events in the marketplace that will have a direct effect, either positive or negative, on the business. However it also includes knowledge about a host of other facts and circumstances that affect the business.

FACTORS TO CONSIDER

The value of a business is derived from many different sources. IRS Revenue Ruling 59-60 identified eight factors that should be considered when determining the value of a closely held company.

The text of Revenue Ruling 59-60 follows.

Rev. Rul. 59-60, 1959-1 CB 237, IRC Sec(s). 2031

Rev. Rul. 59-60, 1959-1 CB 237—IRC Sec. 2031 (Also Section 2512.) (Also Part II, Sections 811(k), 1005, Regulations 105, Section 81.10.)

Code Sec. 2031 Reg. § 20.2031-2

In valuing the stock of closely held corporations, or the stock of corporations where market quotations are not available, all other available financial data, as well as all relevant factors affecting the fair market value must be considered for estate tax and gift tax purposes. No general formula may

be given that is applicable to the many different valuation situations arising in the valuation of such stock. However, the general approach, methods, and factors which must be considered in valuing such securities are
outlined.

Revenue Ruling 54-77, C.B. 1954-1, 187, superseded.

Full Text:

Section 1. Purpose.

The purpose of this Revenue Ruling is to outline and review in general
the approach, methods and factors to be considered in valuing shares of
the capital stock of closely held corporations for estate tax and gift tax
purposes. The methods discussed herein will apply likewise to the valuation of corporate stocks on which market quotations are either unavail-
able or are of such scarcity that they do not reflect the fair market value.

Sec. 2. Background and Definitions.

.01 All valuations must be made in accordance with the applicable provisions of the Internal Revenue Code of 1954 and the Federal Estate Tax
and Gift Tax Regulations. Sections 2031(a), 2032 and 2512(a) of the 1954
Code (sections 811 and 1005 of the 1939 Code) require that the property
to be included in the gross estate, or made the subject of a gift, shall be
taxed on the basis of the value of the property at the time of death of the
decedent, the alternate date if so elected, or the date of gift.

.02 Section 20.2031-1(b) of the Estate Tax Regulations (section 81.10 of
the Estate Tax Regulations 105) and section 25.2512-1 of the Gift Tax
Regulations (section 86.19 of Gift Tax Regulations 108) define fair market value, in effect, as the price at which the property would change hands
between a willing buyer and a willing seller when the former is not under
any compulsion to buy and the latter is not under any compulsion to sell,
both parties having reasonable knowledge of relevant facts. Court decisions frequently state in addition that the hypothetical buyer and seller are
assumed to be able, as well as willing, to trade and to be well informed
about the property and concerning the market for such property.

.03 Closely held corporations are those corporations the shares of which
are owned by a relatively limited number of stockholders. Often the entire stock issue is held by one family. The result of this situation is that little, if any, trading in the shares takes place. There is, therefore, no

established market for the stock and such sales as occur at irregular intervals seldom reflect all of the elements of a representative transaction as defined by the term "fair market value."

Sec. 3. Approach to Valuation.

.01 A determination of fair market value, being a question of fact, will depend upon the circumstances in each case. No formula can be devised that will be generally applicable to the multitude of different valuation issues arising in estate and gift tax cases. Often, an appraiser will find wide differences of opinion as to the fair market value of a particular stock. In resolving such differences, he should maintain a reasonable attitude in recognition of the fact that valuation is not an exact science. A sound valuation will be based upon all the relevant facts, but the elements of common sense, informed judgment and reasonableness must enter into the process of weighing those facts and determining their aggregate significance.

.02 The fair market value of specific shares of stock will vary as general economic conditions change from "normal" to "boom" or "depression," that is, according to the degree of optimism or pessimism with which the investing public regards the future at the required date of appraisal. Uncertainty as to the stability or continuity of the future income from a property decreases its value by increasing the risk of loss of earnings and value in the future. The value of shares of stock of a company with very uncertain future prospects is highly speculative. The appraiser must exercise his judgment as to the degree of risk attaching to the business of the corporation which issued the stock, but that judgment must be related to all of the other factors affecting value.

.03 Valuation of securities is, in essence, a prophecy as to the future and must be based on facts available at the required date of appraisal. As a generalization, the prices of stocks which are traded in volume in a free and active market by informed persons best reflect the consensus of the investing public as to what the future holds for the corporations and industries represented. When a stock is closely held, is traded infrequently, or is traded in an erratic market, some other measure of value must be used. In many instances, the next best measure may be found in the prices at which the stocks of companies engaged in the same or a similar line of business are selling in a free and open market.

Sec. 4. Factors to Consider.

.01 It is advisable to emphasize that in the valuation of the stock of closely held corporations or the stock of corporations where market quotations are either lacking or too scarce to be recognized, all available financial data, as well as all relevant factors affecting the fair market value, should be considered. The following factors, although not all-inclusive are fundamental and require careful analysis in each case:

(a)   The nature of the business and the history of the enterprise from its inception.

(b)   The economic outlook in general and the condition and outlook of the specific industry in particular.

(c)   The book value of the stock and the financial condition of the business.

(d)   The earning capacity of the company.

(e)   The dividend-paying capacity.

(f)   Whether or not the enterprise has goodwill or other intangible value.

(g)   Sales of the stock and the size of the block of stock to be valued.

(h)   The market price of stocks of corporations engaged in the same or a similar line of business having their stocks actively traded in a free and open market, either on an exchange or over-the-counter.

.02 The following is a brief discussion of each of the foregoing factors:

(a)   The history of a corporate enterprise will show its past stability or instability, its growth or lack of growth, the diversity or lack of diversity of its operations, and other facts needed to form an opinion of the degree of risk involved in the business. For an enterprise which changed its form of organization but carried on the same or closely similar operations of its predecessor, the history of the former enterprise should be considered. The detail to be considered should increase with approach to the required date of appraisal, since recent events are of greatest help in predicting the future; but a study of gross and net income, and of dividends covering a long prior period, is highly desirable. The history to be studied should include, but need not be limited to, the nature of the business, its products or services, its operating and investment assets, capital structure, plant facilities, sales records and management, all of which should be considered as of the date of the appraisal, with due regard for recent significant changes. Events of the past that are unlikely to recur in the future should be discounted, since value has a close relation to future expectancy.

(b) A sound appraisal of a closely held stock must consider current and prospective economic conditions as of the date of appraisal, both in the national economy and in the industry or industries with which the corporation is allied. It is important to know that the company is more or less successful than its competitors in the same industry, or that it is maintaining a stable position with respect to competitors. Equal or even greater significance may attach to the ability of the industry with which the company is allied to compete with other industries. Prospective competition, which has not been a factor in prior years, should be given careful attention. For example, high profits due to the novelty of its product and the lack of competition often lead to increasing competition. The public's appraisal of the future prospects of competitive industries or of competitors within an industry may be indicated by price trends in the markets for commodities and for securities. The loss of the manager of a so-called "one-man" business may have a depressing effect upon the value of the stock of such business, particularly if there is a lack of trained personnel capable of succeeding to the management of the enterprise. In valuing the stock of this type of business, therefore, the effect of the loss of the manager on the future expectancy of the business, and the absence of management-succession potentialities are pertinent factors to be taken into consideration. On the other hand, there may be factors which offset, in whole or in part, the loss of the manager's services. For instance, the nature of the business and of its assets may be such that they will not be impaired by the loss of the manager. Furthermore, the loss may be adequately covered by life insurance, or competent management might be employed on the basis of the consideration paid for the former manager's services. These, or other offsetting factors, if found to exist, should be carefully weighed against the loss of the manager's services in valuing the stock of the enterprise.

(c) Balance sheets should be obtained, preferably in the form of comparative annual statements for two or more years immediately preceding the date of appraisal, together with a balance sheet at the end of the month preceding that date, if corporate accounting will permit. Any balance sheet descriptions that are not self-explanatory, and balance sheet items comprehending diverse assets or liabilities, should be clarified in essential detail by supporting supplemental schedules. These statements usually will disclose to the appraiser (1) liquid position (ratio of current assets to current liabilities); (2) gross and net book value of principal classes of fixed assets; (3) working capital; (4) long-term indebtedness; (5) capital structure; and (6) net worth. Consideration also should be given to any assets not essential to the operation of the business, such as investments in securities, real estate, etc. In general, such nonoperating assets will command a lower rate of return than do the operating assets, although in exceptional cases the reverse may be true. In computing the book value per share of stock, assets of the investment type should be revalued on the basis of their market price and the book value adjusted accordingly. Comparison of the company's balance sheets over several years may reveal, among other facts, such developments as the acquisition of additional production facilities or subsidiary companies, improvement in financial position, and details as to recapitalizations and other changes in the capital structure of the corporation. If the corporation has more than one class of stock outstanding, the charter or certificate of incorporation should be examined to ascertain the explicit rights and privileges of the various stock issues including: (1) voting powers, (2) preference as to dividends, and (3) preference as to assets in the event of liquidation.

(d) Detailed profit-and-loss statements should be obtained and considered for a representative period immediately prior to the required date of appraisal, preferably five or more years. Such statements should show (1) gross income by principal items; (2) principal deductions from gross income including major prior items of operating expenses, interest and other expense on each item of long-term debt, depreciation and depletion if such deductions are made, officers' salaries, in total if they appear to be reasonable or in detail if they seem to be excessive, contributions (whether or not deductible for tax purposes) that the nature of its business and its community position require the corporation to make, and taxes by principal items, including income and excess profits taxes; (3) net income available for dividends; (4) rates and amounts of dividends paid on each class of stock; (5) remaining amount carried to surplus; and (6) adjustments to, and reconciliation with, surplus as stated on the balance sheet. With profit and loss statements of this character available, the appraiser should be able to separate recurrent from nonrecurrent items of income and expense, to distinguish between operating income and investment income, and to ascertain whether or not any line of business in which the company is engaged is operated consistently at a loss and might be abandoned with benefit to the company. The percentage of earnings retained for business expansion should be noted when dividend-paying capacity is considered. Potential future income is a major factor in many valuations of closely-held stocks, and all information concerning past income which will be helpful in predicting the future should be secured. Prior earnings records usually are the most reliable guide as to the future expectancy, but resort to arbitrary five-or-ten-year averages without regard to current trends or future prospects will not produce a realistic valuation. If, for instance, a record of progressively increasing or decreasing net income is found, then greater weight may be accorded the most recent years' profits in estimating earning power. It will be helpful, in judging risk and the extent to which a business is a marginal operator, to consider deductions from income and net income in terms of percentage of sales. Major categories of cost and expense to be so analyzed include the consumption of raw materials and supplies in the case of manufacturers, processors and fabricators; the cost of purchased merchandise in the case of merchants; utility services; insurance; taxes; depletion or depreciation; and interest.

(e) Primary consideration should be given to the dividend-paying capacity of the company rather than to dividends actually paid in the past. Recognition must be given to the necessity of retaining a reasonable portion of profits in a company to meet competition. Dividend-paying capacity is a factor that must be considered in an appraisal, but dividends actually paid in the past may not have any relation to dividend-paying capacity. Specifically, the dividends paid by a closely held family company may be measured by the income needs of the stockholders or by their desire to avoid taxes on dividend receipts, instead of by the ability of the company to pay dividends. Where an actual or effective controlling interest in a corporation is to be valued, the dividend factor is not a material element, since the payment of such dividends is discretionary with the controlling stockholders. The individual or group in control can substitute salaries and bonuses for dividends, thus reducing net income and understating the dividend-paying capacity of the company. It follows, therefore, that dividends are less reliable criteria of fair market value than other applicable factors.

(f) In the final analysis, goodwill is based upon earning capacity. The presence of goodwill and its value, therefore, rests upon the excess of net earnings over and above a fair return on the net tangible assets. While the element of goodwill may be based primarily on earnings, such factors as the prestige and renown of the business, the ownership of a trade or brand name, and a record of successful operation over a prolonged period in a particular locality, also may furnish support for the inclusion of intangible value. In some instances it may not be possible to make a separate appraisal of the tangible and intangible assets of the business. The enterprise has a value as an entity. Whatever intangible value there is, which is supportable by the facts, may be measured by the amount by which the appraised value of the tangible assets exceeds the net book value of such assets.

(g) Sales of stock of a closely held corporation should be carefully investigated to determine whether they represent transactions at arm's length. Forced or distress sales do not ordinarily reflect fair market value nor do isolated sales in small amounts necessarily control as the measure of value. This is especially true in the valuation of a controlling interest in a corporation. Since, in the case of closely held stocks, no prevailing market prices are available, there is no basis for making an adjustment for blockage. It follows, therefore, that such stocks should be valued upon a consideration of all the evidence affecting the fair market value. The size of the block of stock itself is a relevant factor to be considered. Although it is true that a minority interest in an unlisted corporation's stock is more difficult to sell than a similar block of listed stock, it is equally true that control of a corporation, either actual or in effect, representing as it does an added element of value, may justify a higher value for a specific block of stock.

(h) Section 2031(b) of the Code states, in effect, that in valuing unlisted securities the value of stock or securities of corporations engaged in the same or a similar line of business which are listed on an exchange should be taken into consideration along with all other factors. An important consideration is that the corporations to be used for comparisons have capital stocks which are actively traded by the public. In accordance with section 2031(b) of the Code, stocks listed on an exchange are to be considered first. However, if sufficient comparable companies whose stocks are listed on an exchange cannot be found, other comparable companies which have stocks actively traded in on the over-the- counter market also may be used. The essential factor is that whether the stocks are sold on an exchange or over-the-counter there is evidence of an active, free public market for the stock as of the valuation date. In selecting corporations for comparative purposes, care should be taken to use only comparable companies. Although the only restrictive requirement as to comparable corporations speci-fied in the statute is that their lines of business be the same or similar, yet it is obvious that consideration must be given to other relevant factors in order that the most valid comparison possible will be ob-tained. For illustration, a corporation having one or more issues of preferred stock, bonds or debentures in addition to its common stock should not be considered to be directly comparable to one having only common stock outstanding. In like manner, a company with a declining business and decreasing markets is not comparable to one with a record of current progress and market expansion.

Sec. 5. Weight to Be Accorded Various Factors.

The valuation of closely held corporate stock entails the consideration of all relevant factors as stated in section 4. Depending upon the circum-stances in each case, certain factors may carry more weight than others because of the nature of the company's business. To illustrate:

(a) Earnings may be the most important criterion of value in some cases whereas asset value will receive primary consideration in others. In general, the appraiser will accord primary consideration to earnings when valuing stocks of companies which sell products or services to the public; conversely, in the investment or holding type of com-pany, the appraiser may accord the greatest weight to the assets un-derlying the security to be valued.

(b) The value of the stock of a closely held investment or real estate holding company, whether or not family owned, is closely related to the value of the assets underlying the stock. For companies of this type the appraiser should determine the fair market values of the as-sets of the company. Operating expenses of such a company and the cost of liquidating it, if any, merit consideration when appraising the relative values of the stock and the underlying assets. The market val-ues of the underlying assets give due weight to potential earnings and dividends of the particular items of property underlying the stock, capitalized at rates deemed proper by the investing public at the date of appraisal. A current appraisal by the investing public should be superior to the retrospective opinion of an individual. For these reasons, adjusted net worth should be accorded greater weight in valuing the stock of a closely held investment or real estate holding company, whether or not family owned, than any of the other customary yardsticks of appraisal, such as earnings and dividend paying capacity.

Sec. 6. Capitalization Rates.

In the application of certain fundamental valuation factors, such as earnings and dividends, it is necessary to capitalize the average or current results at some appropriate rate. A determination of the proper capitalization rate presents one of the most difficult problems in valuation. That there is no ready or simple solution will become apparent by a cursory check of the rates of return and dividend yields in terms of the selling prices of corporate shares listed on the major exchanges of the country. Wide variations will be found even for companies in the same industry. Moreover, the ratio will fluctuate from year to year depending upon economic conditions. Thus, no standard tables of capitalization rates applicable to closely held corporations can be formulated. Among the more important factors to be taken into consideration in deciding upon a capitalization rate in a particular case are: (1) the nature of the business; (2) the risk involved; and (3) the stability or irregularity of earnings.

Sec. 7. Average of Factors.

Because valuations cannot be made on the basis of a prescribed formula, there is no means whereby the various applicable factors in a particular case can be assigned mathematical weights in deriving the fair market value. For this reason, no useful purpose is served by taking an average of several factors (for example, book value, capitalized earnings and capitalized dividends) and basing the valuation on the result. Such a process excludes active consideration of other pertinent factors, and the end result cannot be supported by a realistic application of the significant facts in the case except by mere chance.

Sec. 8. Restrictive Agreements.

Frequently, in the valuation of closely held stock for estate and gift tax purposes, it will be found that the stock is subject to an agreement restricting its sale or transfer. Where shares of stock were acquired by a decedent subject to an option reserved by the issuing corporation to repurchase at a certain price, the option price is usually accepted as the fair market value for estate tax purposes. See Rev. Rul. 54-76, C.B. 1954-1, 194. However, in such case the option price is not determinative of fair market value for gift tax purposes. Where the option, or buy and sell agreement, is the result of voluntary action by the stockholders and is binding during the life as well as at the death of the stockholders, such agreement may or may not, depending upon the circumstances of each case, fix the value for estate tax purposes. However, such agreement is a factor to be considered, with other relevant factors, in determining fair market value. Where the stockholder is free to dispose of his shares during life and the option is to become effective only upon his death, the fair market value is not limited to the option price. It is always necessary to consider the relationship of the parties, the relative number of shares held by the decedent, and other material facts, to determine whether the agreement represents a bonafide business arrangement or is a device to pass the decedent's shares to the natural objects of his bounty for less than an adequate and full consideration in money or money's worth. In this connection see Rev. Rul. 157 C.B. 1953-2, 255, and Rev. Rul. 189, C.B. 1953-2, 294.

Sec. 9. Effect on Other Documents.
    Revenue Ruling 54-77, C.B. 1954-1, 187, is hereby superseded.

The eight factors in Revenue Ruling 59-60 serve as good guidelines:

1. The nature of the business and the history of the enterprise from its inception

2. The economic outlook in general and the condition and outlook of the specific industry in particular

3. The book value of the stock and the financial condition of the business

4. The earnings capacity

5. The dividend-paying capacity

6. Whether or not the enterprise has goodwill or other intangible value

7. Sales of stock and the size of the block of stock to be valued

8. The market price of stocks of corporations engaged in the same or a similar line of business having their stocks actively traded in a free and open market, either on an exchange or over the counter

In this and the following two chapters, we will examine seven of these factors. In the remainder of this chapter, we examine the first two factors: the nature of the business and the economic outlook for its industry.

Because one of the purposes of valuing a business is to determine whether goodwill or other intangible value exists, factor, 6, will not be discussed specifically in this or the next two chapters. Goodwill is typically equal to the value of the entire business in excess of the value of all of the business's other assets, net of liabilities. Goodwill can be a component of the calculated value of a business, which is discussed in Chapter 12. Moreover, Revenue Ruling 65-193 states:

> Revenue Ruling 59-60, C.B. 1959-1, 237, is hereby modified to delete the statements, contained therein at section 4.02(f), that "In some instances it may not be possible to make a separate appraisal of the tangible and intangible assets of the business. The enterprise has a value as an entity. Whatever intangible value there is, which is supportable by the facts, may be measured by the amount by which the appraised value of the tangible assets exceeds the net book value of such assets."
>
> The instances where it is not possible to make a separate appraisal of the tangible and intangible assets of a business are rare and each case varies from the other. No rule can be devised which will be generally applicable to such cases.
>
> Other than this modification, Revenue Ruling 59-60 continues in full force and effect.

Together, the factors in Revenue Ruling 59-60 defining fair market value summarize the information that a potential buyer and you, the seller, need to evaluate a business. To expedite the process, you should compile these data in the selling memo.

THE NATURE OF THE BUSINESS AND ITS HISTORY SINCE INCEPTION

To evaluate your IT business, a buyer must gain a firm understanding of its history, including its origins and evolution to the present. Such an analysis will provide substantial insight into the reasons for its successes and failures; it can also serve as a basis for future projections. A thorough analysis of your business's history with an emphasis on the more recent past will include examinations of its product and service offerings, market position, competition, and relationships with customers, suppliers, and employees.

Through evaluation and due diligence, your potential buyer will attempt to become familiar with the scope and extent of the solutions your business offers. These solutions can include both services and products. Indeed, the solutions a business offers define the company and its relations with competitors and people associated with it, and perhaps define the reason why the business is being sought. Therefore, an understanding of your company's solutions—including potential uses—is a key to assessing its value.

Another component is the business's market position. The way an information technology business is perceived in the market can have a strong impact on its value, both in the present and in the future. One salient perception is whether your business is viewed as a market leader or laggard, innovator or follower, and the level of customer satisfaction that it maintains.

Relationships with customers should also be evaluated. Among the variables usually considered is the likelihood that customers will continue to use your solution. Several factors affect the decision to remain loyal: the overall quality or perceived quality of your solutions; the customers' benefits versus costs; the costs of switching, retooling, retraining; financial and other future prospects; direct and indirect costs; and loss of focus.

You will definitely want, if you have not done so already, to structure your customer relationships, both contractually and practically, to reduce the likelihood of losing established customers upon sale of your business. The best way to maintain this relationship is to ensure your customers appreciate the total value of the underlying relationship and to develop strong relationships in the first place. Ultimately, the buyer will assess the reasons why customers are using your products and services and attempt to determine whether this will continue after the sale. For example, in some cases relationships that defy economic sense have developed through family ties, friendships, or simple convenience.

These are factors that may evaporate once the buyer takes over. Your business's potential value will be increased if it appears these and other relationships can survive and grow after the purchase. Depending on current relationships with customers, therefore, long-term contracts that are easily assignable, or similar initiatives, should be executed prior to your business being marketed, although it must be acknowledged that many long-term contracts will have cancellation clauses for changes in conditions. (And a downside to long-term contracts is that they may limit the buyer's ability to increase prices or redeploy resources.)

Because a buyer will want to assess prospective market share as well as your business's niche and perceived strengths and weaknesses, the purchase price will be increased if this information is not merely positive but documented—not just through customer acceptance but also through awards, citations, independent surveys, and articles authored by outsiders and product reviewers.

Supplier relationships will be evaluated as well. As with customer relationships, a buyer will want to determine whether your business can maintain existing supplier relationships. For example, if your business resells hardware or software, it should have as much flexibility as possible in assigning and modifying suppliers' contracts. Although some buyers may not want to be burdened with long-term contracts at the outset of their ownership, others welcome the security. At the least, most buyers will not want any contracts to lapse immediately upon sale. Written into the purchase/ sale contract can be an initial phase-in period to enable the buyer to become familiar with your business's operations in detail. In the case of takeovers and mergers, however, the newly combined, much larger entity may be able to obtain larger discounts from suppliers due to the increased purchasing power.

Accordingly, you always should try to determine what supplier scenario can reasonably be expected to result in the best outcome.

The most important asset of any IT business is its know-how and ability to execute, which are reflected in the knowledge, experience, and skill of management and employees. A selective buyer will closely evaluate your business's organizational structure, depth of management, and likelihood that current management and key employees will remain on board after the sale. The buyer probably will continually assess how important you and your fellow shareholders are to the business's success. If you and they are deemed to be key employees, an astute buyer probably will craft the offer so a substantial portion of the sale price will be contingent on the business's future results. If the buyer determines that your business has management depth outside of you and the other main shareholders, the portion of the payments that are contingent will decline, and the overall price can increase. The time and expense (including opportunity costs) of replacing an existing key employee typically are steep, a fact very often overlooked within IT companies. You should carefully consider what you, your management team, and the buyer can do following the sale to minimize employee turnover—while giving the acquirer maximum flexibility and comfort level prior to the sale. Not only does this reduce the buyer's risk, it also can increase the sale price. Chapter 5 discusses initiatives that you can implement to retain key people.

THE ECONOMIC OUTLOOK IN GENERAL AND THE CONDITION AND OUTLOOK OF THE INDUSTRY IN WHICH THE BUSINESS OPERATES

External factors naturally can have profound effects on the health of any business. Current strengths and weaknesses, coupled with projections for the economy and the sector(s) your business operates in, purchases from, or sells into, always must be carefully considered. You should try to synthesize some of these data and highlight to the buyer how the conditions that are both general and specific to your company will affect the business and its future. Various economic indicators and performance will have myriad effects on different businesses. You should lay out these variables in a general but forthright manner in your selling memorandum in order to avoid misinterpretation or misrepresentation.

CHAPTER 10

Valuation: Book Value of the Stock and Financial Condition of the Business

In the last chapter, we examined both the standard IRS definition of fair market value and the first two key factors from Revenue Ruling 59-60 in defining that value for a closely held company. In this chapter, we examine the third factor: the book value of the stock and the financial condition of the business.

To assess the financial condition of your business, an evaluator first will analyze its financial statements, which include the balance sheet, profit and loss and cash flow statements, and any changes in financial position.

FINANCIAL STATEMENTS

A potential buyer must have faith in the reliability of your company's financial statements. Reliable statements covering the past 3 to 5 years should not (and typically cannot) be prepared cost-efficiently just before the sale—the process must begin as early as possible in your business's life and continue thereafter.

Although it is preferable to have the higher levels of assurance that an audit (or to a lesser extent a review) provides, many small businesses tend not to conduct audits because of what they perceive is the high cost. If historically your business merely had compilations, in the years prior to the sale it should obtain at the very least a review and preferably an audit. If the business has reviewed financial statements, it should consider obtaining audited statements. In many instances, you will find that the cost of improving the quality of your financial statements is relatively small, even more so when compared with the benefits you ultimately stand to receive. Often the investment can be recouped, because a buyer will almost certainly be willing to pay a higher price for the additional assurance of financial health. Typically you will reap benefits in excess of the fees incurred.

Also, because many information technology businesses have minimal inventory, if any, the accounting work needed to perform a formal audit is significantly reduced as compared with a traditional business that maintains a physical inventory. Personally, I have never had a client complain about the higher costs of improved financial statements after they have sold their business.

A summary of the level of financial statements that a certified public accountant (CPA) can provide—audit, review, and compilation—follows.

Audit

An audited financial statement is the highest level of assurance that a CPA can provide. It involves a review of the business's internal controls, testing of selected transactions and obtaining verification, confirmation, and communication with outside third parties including customers, suppliers, lenders, and attorneys.

At the conclusion of the audit, the CPA's report typically will state that the audit was conducted in accordance with generally accepted accounting principles (GAAP) and the financial statements are fairly stated. The CPA's report does not state the financial statements are free of any errors, as this would be cost-prohibitive.

Review

In a review, the CPA provides limited assurances that the financial statements do not require material modifications to be in conformity with GAAP. It is a lower level of assurance than in an audit, but higher than a compilation. In a review, CPAs typically perform analytical procedures and inquire with the business's management, as well as applying their own knowledge on the business and industry.

Compilation

In a compilation, the CPA prepares the financial statement from information that is provided by the business. The CPA provides no assurance that the financial statements are prepared in conformity with GAAP. This is the lowest level of assurance of the three types of financial statements.

OTHER NON-FINANCIAL DATA

Even an audited statement will not disclose all of the relevant information about a business. For example, it will not disclose nonfinancial issues such as the potential for products under development, the likelihood that key employees will remain with the business after the acquisition, or the strength of customer/supplier relationships. Notwithstanding these limitations, the potential buyer typically will request that the audited financial statement be supplemented by interim financial data from the period covered by the audit through the present.

BALANCE SHEET

Another component of your business's financial health is its balance sheet. When analyzing it, the buyer typically will consider these items:

- Assets
  - Cash
  - Accounts receivable
  - Work in progress
  - Inventory
  - Prepayments
  - Fixed assets (computers, furniture, and equipment)
  - Real estate (land and building)
  - Intangible assets
    - Goodwill
    - Capitalized software as well as research and development costs
  - Investments in other businesses

- Loans to/from shareholders and employees
- Other assets
- Liabilities
  - Payables/accrued liabilities
  - Loans or mortgages payable
  - Prepayments, deferred revenues, and/or deposits
  - Contingent liabilities, including:
    - Warranties and guarantees
      - Lawsuits
      - Audits
      - Compliance with government regulations
  - Other obligations
- Owners' equity
  - Equity
  - Treasury stock

In the remainder of this chapter, we discuss how each of these items contributes to the balance sheet.

Assets

Cash   Although cash may appear to be a bland and unexciting item, your buyer will gauge whether the business operates—and has historically operated—with the appropriate amount of cash. Cash balances can be a double-edged sword for you, the seller. If historically the business has operated with too little cash, management may have been preoccupied with monitoring its current position. It may have spent an inordinate amount of time focusing on the business's short-term liquidity as opposed to efforts that can bolster the business on a long-term basis, such as sales, customer relationships, research and development, hiring new employees, and product development. Moreover, a cash-starved business not only will incur additional interest costs for borrowing money but may also be unwilling to enter into certain contracts and commitments because of the strain that these relationships—including lags in payment—can place on its financial health.

If this is the case, you should explain the lost opportunities to any potential buyer.

Too much cash can have negative implications too. A business with too much cash may not be deploying its assets in the most efficient and productive manner. It may have missed the opportunity to make reinvestments in the business, purchase complementary businesses, raise salaries, or allow the owners to withdraw additional compensation.

In all cases, you should indicate to the buyers what in retrospect you would have done to improve the business: for example, investing in additional marketing and sales activities, reducing turnover, and/or hiring key personnel.

Accounts Receivable   Valuation of receivables is typically one of the most negotiated aspects of a business's sale. You or your staff should carefully analyze the collectibility and age of the receivables. Although there are always variations among industries, and customers' financial condition can have a profound impact on payment policies, the age of receivables beyond a given point is inversely related to customer satisfaction: the lower the age of the receivables, the higher customer satisfaction, and vice versa.

A comparison of the age of receivables over the past few years can provide an indication, in part, of whether overall customer satisfaction has risen or fallen. When this analysis is performed, care should be taken to remove any aberrations or distortions due to overall or sector-specific economic cycles, as industry trends or practices can affect payment cycles. The business's historical collection rate of accounts receivables can provide a good indication of future collections.

Work in Progress   Many information technology businesses do not properly record their work in progress: work that has been performed but not yet billed to clients. Examples might include custom programming, installation services, and training. You should analyze your business's practices to determine if any adjustments are needed. Regardless of whether the business uses a cash or accrual method of accounting for internal reporting, its financial statements may need to be adjusted to reflect such additional assets as accounts receivable, work in progress, accounts payable, and accrued expenses. Accrual basis financial statements usually will provide a more comprehensive picture of the business's financial condition than a cash-basis financial statement. This fact highlights the importance of obtaining, well in advance of a sale, a full understanding of your business's accounting policies and their ramifications to determine if the business's results and financial condition are being accurately portrayed.

QUICK TIP

A simple step to correct the problem of not properly reflecting work in process on its balance sheet may be for the business to bill its clients as the work is being performed as opposed to waiting until the project is complete. Typically a business's cash flow will improve as a result.

Inventory   Even though most businesses today, particularly IT businesses, have little physical inventory, it is still important to value all inventory properly. This process includes adjusting for obsolete goods and for increases or decreases in expected shelf life and pricing of items. Both factors, which are a function of customer demand, can affect the salability of the inventory. Although business practices have evolved toward just-in-time inventory policies, you and others in management always should be vigilant not to purchase slow-moving, excess, or unnecessary inventory. These purchases deplete funds that could be better employed elsewhere and always contain the risk of becoming obsolete.

Prepayments   Prepayments include any item (goods or services) that the business has paid for but not yet received. Prepayments can include goods purchased but not received, as well as prepaid rent, subscriptions, or maintenance fees.

Fixed Assets (Computers, Furniture, Machinery, and Equipment) The book value of a business's computers, furniture, equipment, and machinery as well as any leasehold improvements should be compared with its fair market value. Leasehold improvements include any improvements that are made to leased facilities. Although computers and other technology equipment quickly become obsolete, these assets still can be useful and valuable to the business after they have been fully depreciated and their accounting-determined or tax-determined expected lives have expired. Conversely, these items may be worth less than the value attributed to them on the business's balance sheet, and as a result it may need to be adjusted.

Real Estate (Land and Building)   The book or carrying value of any real estate the company owns should be compared with its fair market value. Typically, the carrying value of real estate purchased many years earlier has been reduced by depreciation on your business's balance sheet, while its market value has continued to grow. (Although the cost of land is not depreciated, the cost of the building and its improvements are depreciated.) On the other hand, the market value of your real estate may have declined due to general or local economic conditions. It can also decrease due to environmental issues, if applicable. You should engage the services of an appraiser or Realtor to value the firm's real estate.

QUICK TIP

Note: Often buyers purchase an IT business for its intellectual capital, not its physical assets. As a result, one option can include selling the business and retaining the real estate (or selling it to a separate buyer).

If you own and retain the real estate after the sale, you will still have a relationship with the buyers as their landlord. A chief disadvantage of this is that the future rental stream will be linked to the fortunes of the new business: If the business does not do well, it may not renew the lease or in the extreme case not be able to pay the rent; if it expands, your buyers may outgrow the space and need to move. There could be other psychological and emotional disadvantages of retaining the real estate: for example, your meddling or anxious watching. You must consider whether you really want to be the business's landlord after the sale.

Intangible Assets   This category includes assets that are not physical. Some examples include trademarks, patents, copyrights, customer lists, or rights. Goodwill, and capitalized software costs, which are discussed below, are intangible assets, too.

Goodwill   Goodwill is the excess of the purchase price over the fair market value of an asset. Your business may reflect goodwill on its balance sheet if it has purchased another entity. As is the case with capitalized software and research and development costs, this treatment may be proper for accounting purposes, but it also may produce an inaccurate or misleading presentation of value. A buyer may remove or adjust the value of this asset from your balance sheet when assessing your business's value.

The FASB issued SFAS 141, which governs financial accounting and reporting for business combinations, and SFAS 142, which governs the financial accounting and reporting for acquired goodwill and other intangibles. SFAS 142 requires the testing of goodwill and indefinite lived intangible assets for impairment as opposed to amortizing them. These pronouncements supercede Accounting Principles Board (APB) 16 and 17, respectively.

Capitalized Software Costs   Pursuant to SFAS No. 86, which was issued by the Financial Accounting Standards Board (FASB), a business can capitalize development costs incurred after software achieves technological feasibility. Many observers feel this treatment may overstate your business's assets as well as distort expenses and income. Accordingly, because a buyer frequently evaluates and assesses these assets to determine whether the values on the balance sheet need to be adjusted, you should continually review your company's practices in these areas.

The summary for SFAS No. 86 states, in part:

> costs incurred internally in creating a computer software product shall be charged to expense when incurred as research and development until technology feasibility has been established for the product. Technological feasibility is established upon completion of a detail program design or, in its absence, completion of a working model. Thereafter, all software production costs shall be capitalized and subsequently reported at the lower of unamortized cost or net realizable value. Capitalized costs are amortized based on current and future revenue for each product with an annual minimum equal to the straight-line amortization over the remaining estimated economic life of the product.[1]

Investments in Other Businesses   If your business has purchased interests in other entities, the fair market value of these investments should be compared with the carrying value of the business. If any of the investments are unrelated to your core business, you should consider selling or transferring these assets out of the core business. You and your financial staff should then recast your business's financial statement to reflect this elimination, both historically and prospectively.

[1]FASB 86

Typically if your business owns less than 20 percent of another business, this investment is accounted under the cost method. If your business exercises significant influence over another business—usually defined as an ownership interest of 20 percent to 50 percent—it is accounted for under the equity method. Under the equity method, the carrying value of the investment is increased or decreased by the proportionate share of the business's income or loss, respectively, and decreased by any dividends received.

Loans to/from Shareholders and Employees   If the transaction is a stock purchase or merger, the purchaser typically will not want to buy a business that owes its shareholders money or to which the shareholders owe money. Loans from the business to shareholders will need to be repaid by the shareholders or recognized as additional compensation. If shareholders have lent money to the business, the buyer will usually request that the obligation be discharged as part of the transaction.

Other Assets   This is a broad classification that can include a wide variety of assets including but not limited to deposits paid by the business, security deposits paid to landlords, and cash value of insurance policies owned by the business.

Liabilities

Payables/Accrued Liabilities   You should analyze your business's balance sheet to determine if all payables and accrued liabilities have been reflected properly. Even though many businesses do not record or accrue for liabilities for which they have not yet received a bill, you as the seller must include these obligations in the balance sheet, because the buyer will undoubtedly ask for a representation that all liabilities have been reflected. Your inclusion of these obligations will reduce the chance that the buyer will improperly value these items and seek a post closing adjustment.

Loans or Mortgages Payable   If your business has obligations in the form of mortgages or loans, they should be reviewed. Among the potential variables that should be considered are:

- Payment terms
- Whether the lender has the right to accelerate payment upon the sale of all or a portion of the business

- Whether the lender would agree to alter the repayment terms, such as the interest rate and repayment period, or reduce the outstanding liability

- Whether the lender will require your ongoing guarantee or additional security, in the form of guarantees or collateral, upon the sale of the business

Prepayments, Deferred Revenues, and/or Deposits   Some business's operating models require customers to pay for services in advance. An example would include prepayments for post contract maintenance or extended support services. Although this practice can provide a welcome funding source, your business should recognize a liability to the customer between the date of payment and the time services are rendered. This liability should be recognized and recorded as income when either the services are performed or the warranty period tolls, but the buyer should be advised of the concomitant cost (which in many cases may be minimal or already reflected in operating expenses).

Contingent Liabilities   These are among the most vexing problems for a buyer analyzing a business. Contingent liabilities are those whose exact amount cannot be reasonably determined, or those that will arise only after a future event. It is important that such potential liabilities be disclosed in clear and concise explanations.

Contingent liabilities can be grouped in four broad categories:

1. *Warranties and guarantees:* A business may have a warranty or guarantee obligation to its customers to refund, repair, or replace a product or service for a period of time following its purchase. In that event, an estimate should be made of the potential cost of this obligation. A business can also have a potential future obligation if it guaranteed the payment of a debt, such as a loan or invoice, by a third party. This obligation materializes only if the primary or prior obligor defaults on it.

2. *Lawsuits:* If your business is party to a lawsuit, it may incur liability as a result of a verdict or negotiated settlement. The potential cost of this liability should be estimated and discussed. A similar adjustment should be made in the case of potential lawsuits or claims, and the likelihood of such suits should also be considered and mentioned.

3. *Audits:* An audit by any government agency, such as the Internal Revenue Service or state department of taxation or revenue, can result in an additional liability assessed against your business. This potential liability should be disclosed.

4. *Compliance with government regulations:* The cost of complying with legal strictures, such as the Department of Labor, Environmental Protection Agency, Occupational Safety Health Administration, Americans with Disabilities Act, and similar federal, state, and local regulations, should be included when calculating liabilities. For a sale, every business must assess its compliance with environmental, ERISA (Employee Retirement Income Security Act), and other laws, even if at first compliance does not seem to be a major issue.

Other Obligations   The impact of other obligations on your balance sheet should be assessed continually.

Owners' Equity

Equity   Equity represents the net worth of a business. It is equal to the difference between the total assets less the total liabilities of the business. Simply stated, owners' equity is also equal to the total investment in the business, which depending on the legal form of the business may be listed as capital or stock (see Exhibit 7.1), plus any income that has been retained by the business, net of distributions, such as dividends to the owners, less any losses.

In any analysis of the equity section of a business's financial statements, the impact of retained earnings as well as your business's legal structure should be evaluated. For example, if the business is organized as a subchapter S or a limited liability corporation (LLC), its accumulated adjustments account or capital, respectively, represent earnings that have already been taxed, in large part, to the business's owner(s), that is, you. If the business is a C corporation, the retained earnings account represents income that has not yet been distributed and taxed to its shareholders; however, it represents the sum total of the business's cumulative, after-tax earnings, net of losses, and dividends since inception. It can be adjusted for recapitalizations, stock dividends, and certain other items.

Treasury Stock   Frequently, if the business is organized as a corporation and has purchased the interest of a prior owner(s), it is reflected as treasury stock. Treasury stock is a contra account and is reflected as a negative adjustment in a business's equity section. You should be fully informed about and prepared to disclose the terms of this transaction, because a prudent buyer will want to review them along with the background and all other related agreements, such as employee contracts, noncompete agreements, and tag-along right, to the transaction.

If a prior shareholder sold his or her interest to an individual or entity other than the corporation, the transaction will not be reflected as treasury stock.

In the next chapter, we discuss another important part of the financial statement—the profit and loss statement—as well as the remaining factors from Revenue Ruling 59-60. The profit and loss statement is key to understanding the earnings capacity of the business. The chapter also includes a discussion of the final two factors in valuing a business: the size of stock to be valued and comparing the stock price with that of similar companies.

CHAPTER 11

The Company's Earnings Capacity: Profit and Loss Statement; Dividend Paying Capacity, The Size of the Block of Stock to be Valued, The Market Price of Similar Stocks

In this chapter, we examine the fourth, fifth, seventh, and eighth factors of Revenue Ruling 59-60:

- The earnings capacity of a company
- The business's dividend-paying capacity
- Sales of stock and the size of the block of stock to be valued
- The market price of stocks of corporations engaged in the same or a similar line of business having their stocks actively traded in a free and open market, either on an exchange or over the counter

THE EARNINGS CAPACITY OF A COMPANY

Analysis of Profit and Loss Statement

Your business's profit and loss (P&L) statement, which summarizes its revenues and expenses, should be analyzed to determine the earnings capacity of the business.

When reviewing revenues, you should consider these questions:

- What portion of the business's revenues is drawn from repeat customers?
- What portion of the revenues is generated by its 10 or 20 largest customers?
- What would happen to the business (in terms of forgone profits) if any of these customers were lost?
- What are the recent trends in terms of revenues—have they grown, remained stable, or declined?
- What are the causes for the change in revenues over the past few years?
- How has the composition of the revenues and the customers that generate them changed over the past few years?
- What are some reasonable assumptions regarding future revenues over the next few years?
- What events could cause revenues to increase or decrease over the next few years?
- What are the greatest risks to the sustainability of revenues?

Similarly, your business's margins and expenses will be analyzed, and these items should be considered:

- What are the margins by region, product, division, and customer set?
- Have there been any variations between the historical and current margins, and if so, why?
- Will margins continue at the current rate, or, if not, what is a reasonable prognosis?
- At your current levels of operation, what are the marginal costs for each additional dollar of revenue?
- How would marginal costs vary at different levels of revenue?

- What expenses are expected to change in the future?

- If your business is introducing a new product, service, or offering, will payroll and other related costs change?

- Conversely, if your business has already introduced a new product, service, or offering, will these costs decline?

- What are the business's fixed costs? What factors can cause them to change?

- Will any macroeconomic factors cause a change in the company's cost structure?

- Will a robust economy, coupled with a tight labor market, cause payroll expenses to rise?

- Will a strong or weak local economy result in an increase or decrease in rental costs?

In many instances, due diligence will focus on historical results, which ignore current events that affect the business. If the business will experience change, and that change can be reasonably predicted, you should bring this to the buyer's attention. For example, if the business's relationships with its largest suppliers or customers evaporate, margins could decline to dangerous levels. Conversely, if new relationships are forged, these margins could improve.

Recasting Your Business's Profit and Loss Statement

For many closely held businesses, the P&L statement does not accurately reflect the expenses that a third party will incur if it owned the business. One salient example concerns the total remuneration of the owner and key employees. If the amount the purchaser would have to pay to these individuals or others who will be performing these functions is more than what the seller is paying, that difference should be deducted from the business's results when calculating its recast profit. Conversely, if the amount the purchaser would have to pay to these individuals or others who will be performing these functions is less than what the seller is paying, that difference should be added to the business's profits when calculating its recast profits. Similarly, the recast P&L statement should reflect any other changes in expenses, such as rent or occupancy, health insurance, retirement plan costs, selling expenses, and/or other costs that will change after the purchase. Other one-time, nonrecurring expenses, such as moving costs, unique marketing campaigns, inventory write-offs, and casualty losses, should also be eliminated.

In sum, the business's recast profit-and-loss statement should reflect as accurately as possible the true cost, to a third party, of running the business. A buyer will base the business's value on what it expects the business to generate in the future. It may perform this calculation by analyzing the business's recent and expected future performance.

Generally the starting point for the recast P&L statement is the business's profit. The profit is then adjusted to reflect these items:

+/– Changes in total remuneration

+/– Changes in rent or other occupancy expenses

+/– Changes in health insurance or retirement plan contributions

+/– Changes in selling and other expenses

+ One-time, nonrecurring expenses for moving, marketing, inventory, write-offs, etc.

+ Discretionary charitable contributions

– One-time, aberrational revenues.

You, as the business owner, should realize that not all of the components in the recast P&L statement will result in an increase to the entity's profit. For example, extraordinary, one-time, or aberrational gains should be removed from the business's income. Moreover, if the new owner will need to pay higher amounts for an existing expense, such as salaries or rent, that increment should be deducted from the business's profit when arriving at the recast figure. (See Exhibit 11.1.)

Typically a business's recast P&L is used as the basis for many of the valuation methods described later in this book.

Notwithstanding the previous discussion, if the business has capitalized software development costs, the potential buyer may analyze the business as if those items were expensed.

THE BUSINESS'S DIVIDEND-PAYING CAPACITY

The business's dividend-paying capacity can also be viewed as the ability, based on its recast pretax income, to pay dividends, whether dividends actually are paid or not.

EXHIBIT 11.1   SAMPLE RECAST PROFIT

	Year 3	Year 2	Year 1
Pretax Income from Financial Statements	$145,000	$100,000	$125,000
Difference between Owners' Remuneration and Remuneration Expense to Be Incurred by Buyer	50,000	40,000	40,000
Difference between Current Rent and Rent to Be Incurred by Buyer	(15,000)	(15,000)	(15,000)
Additional Health Insurance Costs	(12,000)	(12,000)	(12,000)
Selling Expenses That Will Be Eliminated	10,000	9,000	11,000
Nonrecurring Expenses			
Costs of Moving to New Facility	—	—	41,000
Product Brochure (never used)	—	27,500	—
Charitable Contributions	12,000	14,000	15,000
One-time Gain on Sale of Asset	—	(52,000)	—
Recast Pretax Income	$190,000	$111,500	$205,000

SALES OF STOCK AND THE SIZE OF THE BLOCK OF STOCK TO BE VALUED

The size of the stock to be valued refers to whether there is a controlling or noncontrolling interest in the business. It has long been recognized that a minority interest in a business typically will sell for a discount and a majority, controlling interest, for a premium. The next examples illustrate some of the problems that are encountered.

EXAMPLES

Assume two parents start a business and upon their death leave their interest in equal shares to their three children, two of whom are active in the business. The two active children successfully operate the business and draw substantial salaries year after year. In addition, the business also pays for many perquisites, including their health insurance, retirement plans, country club dues, and a healthy dose of travel and entertainment. The nonactive child, who receives no remuneration in any form from the business, attends an annual meeting and inquires why the company does not pay any dividends despite its continuing strong operating results. The active siblings have no desire for the corporation to pay dividends because they are already receiving sufficient remuneration from it and dividends would only result in additional taxation, to both the business and the recipients, even though the dividends are taxed at a lower rate to the individuals. However, as an offering, albeit disingenuous, to the inactive child, they encourage that this matter be brought to a vote of the shareholders. As expected, the motion for dividends is defeated two to one. Similar results occur on other proposals brought forward by the inactive sibling.

Assuming that everyone agrees that the value of the entire business is $6 million, would any reasonable purchaser pay $2 million (1/3 × $6 million) for the inactive sibling's interest? The difference between the purchase price that one would pay for the inactive sibling's interest and $2 million is the minority interest discount in this case.

Now, consider how the answer would change if there was a realistic expectation the business would be sold in the not-too-distant future and the existing owners would receive a portion of the payment equal to their proportionate interest in the business.

QUICK TIP

Assume there is another closely held business where there are three shareholders, owning 47 percent, 47 percent, and 6 percent of the stock. The two 47 percent shareholders have diametrically different views about the business; they disagree about most matters concerning its operations. Assuming that a simple majority is needed to effect any changes in the business, the stock owned by the 6 percent shareholder is needed to pass any motions. As a result, the stock of the 6 percent shareholder probably will not be subject to the normal minority interest discount and in certain circumstances may be able to command a majority premium, especially if the two remaining shareholders were competing to purchase it.

EXAMPLE

Assume there is a closely held business with two shareholders, one owning 80 percent of the stock and the other owning the remaining 20 percent. If someone were to purchase the interest of the 80 percent shareholder, the person probably would be willing to pay a majority premium for it, because he or she would control the business. The majority premium could be no more than an additional 20 percent of the total value of the business (which amounts to 25 percent of the 80 percent: 20 / 80 = 25%).

One method to determine an appropriate minority discount is to analyze the change in value of publicly held stocks that were subject to a takeover. The basis for this comparison is that an owner of a publicly held stock purchases a minority interest in a business. In a takeover, the acquirer is seeking to obtain control of the business. The difference in price between what

[1]Pratt, Shannon P., Reilly F., Schweihs, Robert P., Valuing a Business: The Analysis and Appraisal of Closely Held Companies Fourth Edition, McGraw-Hill, 2000, pp. 353–360.

the security traded for prior to the announcement of the proposed takeover and the actual takeover price as compared to the stock's price can be another data point in calculating the minority discount.[1] Overall merger and acquisition market and industry premiums are published by FactSet Mergerstat, LLC in the *Mergerstat Review* and aggregate, industry and transaction premiums are available in the *Mergerstat Premium Study*.

A shareholders' or other agreement among the owners of the business granting one or more of them additional or less rights, such as supermajority rights, would be a salient point when considering if a majority premium or a minority discount should be applied. Supermajority rights require a vote in excess of one-half to approve certain decisions. Supermajority rights effectively grant minority owners the power to veto or approve acts of the business.

Revenue Ruling 93-12 also discussed the issue of a minority discount. It stated:

Part I

Section 2512. — Valuation of Gifts

26 CFR 25.2512-1: Valuation of property; in general.

ISSUE

If a donor transfers shares in a corporation to each of the donor's children, is the factor of corporate control in the family to be considered in valuing each transferred interest, for purposes of section 2512 of the Internal Revenue Code?

FACTS

P owned all of the single outstanding class of stock of X corporation. P transferred all of P's shares by making simultaneous gifts of 20 percent of the shares to each of P's five children, A, B, C, D, and E.

LAW AND ANALYSIS

Section 2512(a) of the Code provides that the value of the property at the date of the gift shall be considered the amount of the gift.

Section 25.2512-1 of the Gift Tax Regulations provides that, if a gift is made in property, its value at the date of the gift shall be considered the amount of the gift. The value of the property is the price at which the property would change hands between a willing buyer and a willing seller, neither being under any compulsion to buy or to sell, and both having reasonable knowledge of relevant facts.

Section 25.2512-2(a) of the regulations provides that the value of stocks and bonds is the fair market value per share or bond on the date of the gift. Section 25.2512-2(f) provides that the degree of control of the business represented by the block of stock to be valued is among the factors to be considered in valuing stock where there are no sales prices or bona fide bid or asked prices.

Rev. Rul. 81-253, 1981-1 C.B. 187, holds that, ordinarily, no minority shareholder discount is allowed with respect to transfers of shares of stock between family members if, based upon a composite of the family members' interests at the time of the transfer, control (either majority voting control or de facto control through family relationships) of the corporation exists in the family unit. The ruling also states that the Service will not follow the decision of the Fifth Circuit in Estate of Bright v. United States, 658 F.2d 999 (5th Cir. 1981).

In Bright, the decedent's undivided community property interest in shares of stock, together with the corresponding undivided community property interest of the decedent's surviving spouse, constituted a control block of 55 percent of the shares of a corporation. The court held that, because the community-held shares were subject to a right of partition, the decedent's own interest was equivalent to 27.5 percent of the outstanding shares and, therefore, should be valued as a minority interest, even though the shares were to be held by the decedent's surviving spouse as trustee of a testamentary trust. See also, Propstra v. United States, 680 F.2d 1248 (9th Cir. 1982). In addition, Estate of Andrews v. Commissioner, 79 T.C. 938 (1982), and Estate of Lee v. Commissioner, 69 T.C. 860 (1978), nonacq., 1980-2 C.B. 2, held that the corporation shares owned by other family members cannot be attributed to an individual family member for determining whether the individual family member's shares should be valued as the controlling interest of the corporation.

After further consideration of the position taken in Rev. Rul. 81-253, and in light of the cases noted above, the Service has concluded that, in the case of a corporation with a single class of stock, notwithstanding the family relationship of the donor, the donee, and other shareholders, the shares of other family members will not be aggregated with the transferred shares to determine whether the transferred shares should be valued as part of a controlling interest.

In the present case, the minority interests transferred to A, B, C, D, and E should be valued for gift tax purposes without regard to the family relationship of the parties.

HOLDING

If a donor transfers shares in a corporation to each of the donor's children, the factor of corporate control in the family is not considered in valuing each transferred interest for purposes of section 2512 of the Code. For estate and gift tax valuation purposes, the Service will follow Bright, Propstra, Andrews, and Lee in not assuming that all voting power held by family members may be aggregated for purposes of determining whether the transferred shares should be valued as part of a controlling interest. Consequently, a minority discount will not be disallowed solely because a transferred interest, when aggregated with interests held by family members, would be a part of a controlling interest. This would be the case whether the donor held 100 percent or some lesser percentage of the stock immediately before the gift.

EFFECT ON OTHER DOCUMENTS

Rev. Rul. 81–253 is revoked. Acquiescence is substituted for the nonacquiescence in issue one of Lee, 1980-2 C.B. 2.

MARKET PRICE OF COMPARABLE STOCKS

The market price of stocks of corporations engaged in the same or a similar line of business having their stocks actively traded in a free and open market, either on an exchange or over the counter is another method of determining a business's value.

This method is also referred to as the guideline publicly traded company method. This process entails locating publicly traded companies that are similar to the company being valued. There are many characteristics to consider when comparing companies. Among the factors are the markets being served, solutions offered, management and organizational depth, revenues, earnings, book value, capital and debt structure, and dividend-paying capacity.[2] After locating and analyzing the companies to determine if they are truly comparable, the metrics of the guideline companies should be

[2]Ibid, 230.

compared to the business being valued. Some metrics can include the price/earnings multiple, cash flow multiple, price-to-book multiple, and price-to-sales multiple. It is important to remember that the price of publicly traded stocks represents a minority interest in the business. That fact should be kept in mind when considering any value derived from these metrics. A discount for lack of marketability (DLOM) typically is applied when comparing a privately held company to a public company.

CHAPTER 12

Methods of Determining a Business's Value

In the last three chapters, we discussed seven vital components to consider when valuing a business. In this final chapter on valuation, we compare specific valuation methods. Several different ones can be used depending on the facts and circumstances as well as the available data, some more appropriate or expedient to utilize than others. Some of these methods include:

- Comparable sales
- Revenue or sales multiple
- Earnings multiple
- Cash flow multiple
- Discounted cash flow
- Capitalization of excess income/excess earnings
- Replacement cost

This chapter briefly discusses these methods, along with their strengths and weaknesses. All valuation methods rely on a variety of assumptions that should be carefully considered throughout the valuation process. In many cases, a buyer may base the valuation on what the business is expected to generate over the foreseeable future. As a result, the recast P&L, as modified, may be utilized. Two other valuation methods—book value and liquidation value—do not assign any value to the business's future income stream or cash flow. The book value method values the business as being equal to the assets less liabilities, as reflected on its financial statements. The liquidation value method assumes the business's assets are being sold at a forced sale and deducts the liabilities against this amount.

Prior to proceeding, two terms that are frequently utilized when valuing businesses are the capitalization rate and the discount rate. The capitalization rate is a divisor, which is typically expressed as a percentage, which is used to convert the anticipated economic benefits of a single period into a value. The discount rate is a rate of return that is typically expressed in the form of a percentage, which is used to convert a future monetary sum or sums into a present value[1].

COMPARABLE SALES

One method to gauge the value of an information technology company is to compare it with similar companies that have recently been sold or any recent sales of the company's stock. When utilizing other companies, it is important to select truly comparable companies, if possible, and make appropriate adjustments for differences. Many prefer this method when evaluating a closely held business. However, the challenge in utilizing and applying this method is locating closely held and publicly held companies that are truly comparable to the target business that is being valued.

Some companies may appear similar but in fact use different business models. Moreover, they may use different accounting policies, which can render all comparisons meaningless unless adjustments are made to eliminate the distortions. Finally, the valuation of items including accounts receivable, inventory, and payables as well as assumption of various debts is negotiated during the course of the purchase. Differences in these items' valuations will have a profound effect on a business's value. All of these factors can alter the comparability of companies. Moreover, in addition to the stated purchase price, the owner(s) may receive deferred compensation from the buyer, which must be considered when comparing one business to the other.

Another important valuation variable is whether your business owns the real estate it occupies or, if not, whether its lease terms are favorable.

Once truly comparable cohort companies have been selected for analysis, it is vitally important to obtain all of the necessary information to permit a meaningful and thorough comparison.

---

[1]Pratt, Shannon P. Business Valuation Body of Knowledge Second Edition, John Wiley and Sons, Inc. page 73

It should also be remembered that the companies selected as being comparable may have sold for a price that did not reflect their value, the market may have changed since the sale, or other factors may have significantly affected the price.

Finding a publicly traded company for comparison presents a special challenge. Similarities obviously must go beyond simply having the same NAICS number (North American Industry Classification System). (NAICS has replaced Standard Industrial Classification [SIC] codes.) Differences in size, customer concentration, product offerings, geographic markets, management as well as organizational depth and access to capital can render two apparently similar companies incomparable. It is extremely important, then, to have a full understanding of the business(es) you (or your consultants) want to use for comparisons.

Assuming two companies are similar, a discount for lack of marketability (DLOM) is typically applied when comparing a closely held business with a public one. An owner of a publicly held business can sell his or her interest on any business day and receive the proceeds three business days later; the same does not apply to the owner of a closely held business, who frequently must wait months or years to be paid for his or her interest. This may not always apply to owners of large interests in publicly held businesses, in which a blockage discount should be calculated and applied if possible, or if the shareholder owns restricted or "lettered" stock, which cannot be sold until the expiration of a stated time period.

Recent sales of the company's stock may provide an indication of value. However, you should examine the details and circumstances surrounding this transaction carefully, and ascertain:

- Was the transaction made at "arm's length?"

- Has the business changed since the transaction occurred? Was the transaction in the recent past? Is it too remote in time to be meaningful?

- Does the payment for the stock represent the entire consideration paid? For example, the seller may have also received an employment contract, a consulting contract, as well as deferred compensation. All of these items should be evaluated when calculating the total consideration paid for the stock.

- Was a minority or majority interest purchased? If so, the value may need to be adjusted to allow for the minority discount or majority premium.

- Was the buyer a "forced" buyer or the seller a "forced" seller? Was the buyer so anxious to purchase or the seller so anxious to sell that the price paid was above or below fair market value?
- Was the price based on a long-standing agreement that was not updated as the business evolved?

REVENUE OR SALES MULTIPLE

This book has already discussed some of the strengths and weaknesses of relying on a multiple or percentage of revenues, the formula most business owners utilize when arriving at the value of their business. As a result, even if you do not use the Revenue or Sales multiple, you should convert the arrived-upon value into a sales multiple or percentage, as often this is the term or metric that buyers may best understand. Part of the reason for the wide fluctuation in the business's values as a multiple or percentage of sales is the wide disparity of income, cash flow, net assets (assets less liabilities), potential, and other benefits at comparable levels of sales.

This non-IT example illustrates this concept.

CASE STUDY

PROBLEMS WITH REVENUE OR SALES MULTIPLE

Two gas stations are located across the street from each other in the same town. Every year they sell virtually the same number of gallons of gas at the same prices and generate the same gross revenues and gross margins. The labor costs at both stations are virtually identical. But one gas station has been at the same location 20 years longer than the other, and its monthly rent is significantly lower. Assuming both leases will continue for a decade or more and can be assumed by the buyers, a purchase price based on gross revenue or gross margin would severely understate the value of one gas station and overstate the value of the other.

EARNINGS MULTIPLE

One of the most widely used metrics to calculate the value of publicly held businesses is the price/earnings (P/E) multiple. This metric indicates the relationship between a company's stock price and its earnings per share.

On the surface, this method is relatively simple: applying a multiple of the business's adjusted earnings whether they are EBIT (earnings before interest and taxes) or EBITDA (earnings before interest, taxes, depreciation, and amortization) to arrive at its value. However, this method is reliable only if comparable companies (comps) with appropriate adjustments are utilized when calculating the multiple.

Over the last few years, there has been substantial variation in this multiple as it relates to privately held companies and more specifically among IT and other businesses in high-growth areas. Businesses that have exhibited sustained growth in the past and expect rapid growth in the future, and encounter decreasing marginal costs, can expect to sell for more, all other factors being the same, than businesses that do not enjoy these benefits.

EXPLANATION

An earnings multiple of five translates into a capitalization rate of 20 percent (1/5 = 20%); an earnings multiple of four and six translates into capitalization rates of 25 percent (1/4 = 25%) and 16.66 percent (1/6 = 16.66%), respectively. The higher the capitalization rate, the lower the multiple, and vice versa.

CASH FLOW MULTIPLE

The cash flow multiple is similar to the earning multiple except it is based on the cash generated by the business. Many closely held business owners (and others including appraisers, valuation professionals, and financial analysts) view EBITDA, which can be seen as a modified cash flow calculation, as an important determinant. However, capital expenditures are not deducted when calculating EBITDA.

At times the question arises whether the business's earnings and cash flow should be calculated before or after deducting income taxes. It is this author's belief that the question should be viewed from a common-sense prospective: If the pretax earnings or cash flow are utilized, a lower multiple or higher capitalization rate should be employed; if the after-tax earnings and cash flow are utilized, a higher multiple or lower capitalization rate should be employed.

However, as was the case with the earnings multiple method, care should be taken when arriving at the appropriate multiple.

DISCOUNTED CASH FLOW

In the discounted cash flow (DCF) method, the business's earnings for the next few years are projected and discounted to the present in order to calculate the present value. The major variables in calculating the value using this formula are the business's cash flow over the next several years as well as the discount rate that should be utilized. The projected cash flow is calculated based on reasonable assumptions concerning performance. These assumptions include revenues, revenue growth, gross margins, operating expenses, tax rates, capital expenditures (CAPEX), depreciation, working capital requirements, and growth of accounts receivable and accounts payable. The discount rate is composed of the risk-free rate plus a risk component. The risk component includes factors that reflect these risks: business, financial, liquidity, industry, geographic, political, and foreign exchange.

Many believe the DCF provides a logical method to value a business based on its future projections. However concerns about the DCF include the fact that the underlying assumptions and a slight change in these assumptions can have a profound effect on the ultimate results, more than with other valuation criteria and methods. Moreover, the terminal value typically can represent two-thirds or more of the total value.

Exhibit 12.1 calculates the firm and equity value of a hypothetical business utilizing the DCF method. The equity value is equal to the firm value, or value of the invested capital, less the interest-bearing debt.

The DCF method typically assumes a variable income stream over the next three to seven years and thereafter a constant income stream. A variation of this method is the capitalization of earnings method, which utilizes the same methodology as the DCF method but includes a constant income stream for the duration of the calculation period.

CAPITALIZATION OF EXCESS INCOME/EXCESS EARNINGS

The Internal Revenue Service has promulgated a method for the capitalization of excess income/excess earnings, which is discussed in Revenue Ruling 68-609. Pursuant to this method, the business's weighted average income, before owners' compensation and taxes and preferably over the last five years, is reduced by a reasonable compensation for the owner(s) and then by income taxes. Thereafter, the income is reduced by a percentage return on the value of its net assets. (Net assets are the business's assets less its liabilities.) The percentage return is defined in the ruling as "the percentage prevailing in the industry involved at the date of valuation, or (when the industry percentage is not available) a percentage of 8 to 10 percent may be used." This difference, deemed to be earnings from intangible assets or "excess" income, is capitalized at a rate based on the combination of the risk-free rate plus the risk component. The business's fair market value under this method equals the net assets plus the capitalized excess income.

However, prior to utilizing this method, you should keep in mind the third to last paragraph of this pronouncement:

> Accordingly, the "formula" approach may be used for determining the fair market value of intangible assets of a business only if there is no better basis therefore available.[2]

The steps to perform this process are summarized in Exhibit 12.2.

The excess owners' remuneration, which is defined as the amount the owners are paid beyond what would have been paid to a third party, performing the same services, should be added back to the business's income. Conversely, if you, as the owner, are receiving less than what would have been paid to a third party, the difference should be deducted from the business's income.

Revenue Ruling 68-609 in its entirety follows.

Rev. Rul. 68-609, 1968-2 CB 327, IRC Sec(s). 1001

> The "formula" approach may be used in determining the fair market value of intangible assets of a business only if there is no better basis available for

[2]IRS Revenue Ruling 68-609

EXHIBIT 12.1 SAMPLE DCF CALCULATION

For Illustrative Purposes Only

Revenue	$7,000,000
Cost of Goods Sold	30%
Fixed Expenses	15%
Variable Expenses	20%
Interest Expense	0.1%
Income Taxes	40%
Accounts Receivable	5%
Accounts Payable	2%
Depreciation	0.3%
Net Working Capital	6%
Capital Expenditures	2%
Growth Rate Yrs. 1–4	6%
Terminal Growth Rate	3%
Discount Rate	19%

		Year 1	Year 2	Year 3	Year 4	Terminal Value
Revenue		$7,000,000	$7,420,000	$7,865,200	$8,337,112	
Cost of Goods Sold		(2,100,000)	(2,226,000)	(2,359,560)	(2,501,134)	
Fixed Expense		(1,050,000)	(1,113,000)	(1,179,780)	(1,250,567)	
Variable Expense		(1,400,000)	(1,484,000)	(1,573,040)	(1,667,422)	
Interest Expense		(7,000)	(7,420)	(7,865)	(8,337)	
Net Income before Taxes		2,443,000	2,589,580	2,744,955	2,909,652	
Less: Income Taxes	40%	(977,200)	(1,035,832)	(1,097,982)	(1,163,861)	
Net Income after Taxes		$1,465,800	$1,553,748	$1,646,973	$1,745,791	
Cash Flow Adjustments						
Interest Expense	Add	$7,000	$7,420	$7,865	$8,337	
Noncash Charges (Deferred Taxes)	Add	2,500	1,800	900	1,200	
Depreciation and Amortization	Add	21,000	22,260	23,596	25,011	
Change in Working Capital Requirements	Subtract	—	(25,200)	(26,712)	(28,315)	
Capital Expenditures	Subtract	(140,000)	(148,400)	(157,304)	(166,742)	
Cash Flow to Invested Capital		$1,356,300	$1,411,628	$1,495,318	$1,585,283	$10,205,258
Present Value Factor Based on Discount Rate of 19% Assuming Midyear Convention		$1,243,318	$1,087,426	$967,979	$862,367	$5,551,491
Total Value of Firm						9,712,582
Less: Market Value of Interest-Bearing Debt						(3,000,000)
Value of Equity						$6,712,582

EXHIBIT 12.2 CAPITALIZATION OF EXCESS INCOME

	Line	Year 1	Year 2	Year 3	Year 4	Year 5	Formula
Normalization of Income							
Normalized Income before Taxes and Deducting Reasonable Compensation	A						
Less: Reasonable Compensation	B						
Normalized Income before Taxes	C						A − B
Less: Income Taxes	D						
Normalized Income after Taxes	E						C − D
Calculation of Weighted Average							
Weight	F	5	4	3	2	1	
Weighted Income	G						E × F
Total Weighted Income	H						Sum of G
Divided by	I					15	Sum of F
Weighted Average Income after Taxes	J						H / I

Return on Net Assets

Net Assets as Adjusted	K	
Rate of Return on Net Assets	L	
Return on Net Assets	M	$K \times L$

Summary

Excess Income	N	$J - M$
Capitalization Rate	O	
Capitalized Value of Excess Income	P	N / O
Net Assets	Q	K
Total Value	R	$P + Q$

making the determination; A.R.M. 34, A.R.M. 68, O.D. 937, and Revenue Ruling 65-192 superseded.

Full Text:

The purpose of this Revenue Ruling is to update and restate, under the current statute and regulations, the currently outstanding portions of A.R.M. 34, C.B. 2, 31 (1920), A.R.M. 68, C.B. 3, 43 (1920), and O.D. 937, C.B. 4, 43 (1921).

The question presented is whether the "formula" approach, the capitalization of earnings in excess of a fair rate of return on net tangible assets, may be used to determine the fair market value of the intangible assets of a business

The "formula" approach may be stated as follows:

A percentage return on the average annual value of the tangible assets used in a business is determined, using a period of years (preferably not less than five) immediately prior to the valuation date. The amount of the percentage return on tangible assets, thus determined, is deducted from the average earnings of the business for such period and the remainder, if any, is considered to be the amount of the average annual earnings from the intangible assets of the business for the period. This amount (considered as the average annual earnings from intangibles), capitalized at a percentage of, say, 15 to 20 percent, is the value of the intangible assets of the business determined under the "formula" approach.

The percentage of return on the average annual value of the tangible assets used should be the percentage prevailing in the industry involved at the date of valuation, or (when the industry percentage is not available) a percentage of 8 to 10 percent may be used.

The 8 percent rate of return and the 15 percent rate of capitalization are applied to tangibles and intangibles, respectively, of businesses with a small risk factor and stable and regular earnings; the 10 percent rate of return and 20 percent rate of capitalization are applied to businesses in which the hazards of business are relatively high.

The above rates are used as examples and are not appropriate in all cases. In applying the "formula" approach, the average earnings period and the capitalization rates are dependent upon the facts pertinent thereto in each case.

The past earnings to which the formula is applied should fairly reflect the probable future earnings. Ordinarily, the period should not be less than five years, and abnormal years, whether above or below the average, should be eliminated. If the business is a sole proprietorship or partnership, there should be deducted from the earnings of the business a reasonable amount for services performed by the owner or partners engaged in the business. See *Lloyd B. Sanderson Estate v. Commissioner,* 42 F. 2d 160 (1930). Further, only the tangible assets entering into net worth, including accounts and bills receivable in excess of accounts and bills payable, are used for determining earnings on the tangible assets. Factors that influence the capitalization rate include (1) the nature of the business, (2) the risk involved, and (3) the stability or irregularity of earnings.

The "formula" approach should not be used if there is better evidence available from which the value of intangibles can be determined. If the assets of a going business are sold upon the basis of a rate of capitalization that can be substantiated as being realistic, though it is not within the range of figures indicated here as the ones ordinarily to be adopted, the same rate of capitalization should be used in determining the value of intangibles.

Accordingly, the "formula" approach may be used for determining the fair market value of intangible assets of a business only if there is no better basis therefor available.

See also Revenue Ruling 59-60, C.B. 1959-1, 237, as modified by Revenue Ruling 65-193, C.B. 1965-2, 370, which sets forth the proper approach to use in the valuation of closely-held corporate stocks for estate and gift tax purposes. The general approach, methods, and factors, outlined in Revenue Ruling 59-60, as modified, are equally applicable to valuations of corporate stocks for income and other tax purposes as well as for estate and gift tax purposes. They apply also to problems involving the determination of the fair market value of business interests of any type, including partnerships and proprietorships, and of intangible assets for all tax purposes.

A.R.M. 34, A.R.M. 68, and O.D. 937 are superseded, since the positions set forth therein are restated to the extent applicable under current law in this Revenue Ruling. Revenue Ruling 65-192, C.B. 1965-2, 259, which contained restatements of A.R.M. 34 and A.R.M. 68, is also superseded.

REPLACEMENT COST METHOD

The replacement cost method seeks to determine the cost of duplicating the offerings of the business. However, whenever calculating the business's value based on the replacement cost method, you should consider the additional value of having the offerings available immediately versus sometime in the future. In addition, the value of a subsequent corrected and updated iteration of the offering versus the initial version should also be factored into the equation. Many customers are reluctant to purchase the initial version (version 1.0) of a product since it is new, untested, and many of the problems have not been corrected.

Business people frequently perform a make versus buy decision, comparing the cost of developing the product internally versus purchasing an existing, working solution. The replacement value calculates the costs of recreating the business's costs of development that can include the sum of the following:

- Direct employee and subcontractor costs of developing solution(s)
- Indirect employee and subcontractor costs of developing solution(s)
- Selling, general and administrative costs that would be incurred
- Costs for any other assets, net of liabilities, that are being purchased

SPECIAL VALUATION CONSIDERATIONS OF IT BUSINESSES

In today's dynamic economy, a business's valuation can change more rapidly than ever, and this is particularly true with an IT business. A buyer always will consider projected revenues and expenses, but often the purchase is being contemplated for its synergistic potential, as discussed earlier. In this case, the buyer's projections, which you will not always be privy to, will obviously consider the potential of the entity either on a stand-alone basis or combined with the buyer's other business(es).

Irrational exuberance aside, one reason publicly traded technology (and other) stocks may have been valued at all-time highs a few years ago, and have come down to much lower levels since, is that the historical data used to monitor business performance have not evolved to reflect important changes that occurred. In today's world, the greatest assets of most businesses continue to be superior technology, skilled employees, and brands. However, the costs of acquiring and improving these assets typically are expensed in the form of salaries and related costs. This is in contrast to the acquisition of machinery and equipment, which is capitalized and expensed over long periods of time. The divergent accounting treatment afforded the acquisition of physical assets versus human and intellectual capital can cause the multiples afforded IT companies to seem high to the untrained eye, quite apart from investor and shareholder sentiment.[3]

Accounting rules typically require the recognition of expense at the time salaries are earned (although there are exceptions). This reduces a business's earnings and may understate its assets. Popular stock market measurements in addition to the price to earnings ratio or P/E multiple are the price-to-book (P/B) multiple, the company's price per share divided by its book value per share; and the price-to-sales (P/S) multiple, which is the ratio of the company's price per share divided by its sales per share. It is incumbent upon you, the selling business owner, to advise your purchasers (or, in other situations, your investors or lenders) of the effect that accounting short-comings may have on your financial results.

Intellectual Property

Sometimes during the transactions surrounding a business sale, questions arise or stipulations are made about patents and other intellectual property (IP) as an independent factor to be evaluated. Trademarks, service marks, copyrights, and patents typically are already included in the negotiation, but more substantive IP assets are on occasion deemed, or argued to be, a separate matter, with their own life, future, and worth. This is especially true if these assets can be sold separately and not impact the existing business or can be the nucleus for another business or business segment

It is this writer's experience and judgment, however, that IP valuation is best done empirically and not abstractly or wishfully. In other words, evaluate your IP based on its effect on the actual business, your cash flow, earnings, and revenues, just as you would any other asset of the business.

It is, however, important that the business own or control all of its assets, especially IP. As a result, it is important that any business, whether contemplating a sale or not, appropriately registers and protects its assets throughout its existence. This is best done with an IP attorney.

Moreover, every business should have a provision in its employee manual and employment agreements stating that anything an employee develops, as it relates to his or her work, is owned by the business. A similar provision

[3]Wall Street Journal November 3, 1997 Op-Ed article by Lowell L. Bryan

should be included in all contracts with independent contractors and independent contractors' subcontractors. As the laws vary by jurisdiction and also evolve over time, it is always best to consult with a local IP attorney.

Real Estate

If the business or a related party, such as the owner(s), own the real estate that the company occupies, and it is being sold, it must be appraised to determine its value. In addition to determining its fair market value, its fair rental value should be determined. The fair rental value will be needed in the event the business leases the property and a recast financial statement is being furnished, or if the new owner(s) will be leasing the real estate from the seller(s) or a related party.

CHAPTER 13

Confidentiality: An Introduction

One of the major concerns faced by you as the seller of an information technology business is protecting confidential information. This information includes not just your intellectual property—your technology and software programs and processes—but customer lists, trade secrets, marketing plans, and overall ways of doing business. All of this information could be of use to your competitors. Naturally you will be wary of revealing such information to anyone outside the company. But potential buyers must have a clear and full picture of what they are about to purchase.

This and the next chapter offer some guidance about how to minimize the risk of supplying information to potential buyers. In this chapter, we examine the need for confidentiality when competitors are the potential buyers; how to determine the intent of certain buyers; how to evaluate different buyers; disclosing financial information; and how and when to involve your employees in the sale. In the next chapter, we examine how to limit dissemination of data; how to prepare a confidentiality agreement; and practical advice on how to keep a negotiation confidential.

COMPETITORS AS BUYERS

Among the most likely potential buyers of any IT business are existing competitors. But likely buyers can also include potential future competitors too: Your suppliers and customers, also likely buyers, could become competitors later on. In the event that a sale is negotiated but not consummated, all these parties could reap undue advantage through learning vital information about your company, from intellectual property to customer names, pricing, and sales volumes. Allowing such information to slip into the wrong hands can severely damage a company's competitiveness. The risk of losing key customers is substantial, so you must take seriously the problem and potential exposure.

However, it is reasonable for buyers to request information about a company they are considering. They are justified in wanting to know whether your company is in good financial shape and has solid relationships with customers, suppliers, and employees, and whether this situation is likely to continue. They have a right to certain information about your products and other offerings and to know whether those products and services can be expected to keep the company competitive in coming years and whether they perform as promised. To anyone considering buying the business, the more information gathered the better. And when the buyer's advisors and employees are providing assistance or counsel, they too need to obtain sufficient data before making recommendations.

There is no universal solution to the quandary you are in as seller and no way to completely avoid the associated risks. However, you can take certain precautions.

Determining Intent

You always must be alert to the possibility that your suitor is disingenuous. From the very first interaction, you must continually assess whether a potential buyer is unscrupulous or whether the need to obtain information is legitimate.

In addition, many potential buyers are the ultimate tire kickers, meaning they continually look at businesses to purchase but do not make the actual purchase. They may not be intentionally disingenuous, but they look at many businesses, request substantial data (much of which may be unnecessary or burdensome to gather), and rarely make the purchase. In the process, these individuals learn a lot about your company, subject you to unnecessary work, and cause you to divert attention from operating your business. They may even distract you from dealing with legitimate buyers, resulting in substantial opportunity costs for you and your business.

Although there is no foolproof method for ascertaining buyer motives, there are several steps you should take before you provide detailed information to anyone.

- Although it will sound obvious, spend some time talking with the buyer and his or her advisors in person. Observe carefully to see how they, especially the principal, conduct themselves and their own business, to try to determine if they are sincere about purchasing yours. As with any personal interaction, be alert for warning signs.

- Try to learn if you and the buyer have mutual acquaintances who might provide you with a reference or other information.

- Examine the buyer's history. Has he or she purchased businesses in the past? What is his or her reputation, and how has he or she conducted himself or herself during past deals?

Some buyers are known for being very honest and candid; others have a far different reputation. Obtaining as much of this information as possible will help you avoid a bad experience.

First-time Buyers

Keep in mind that just because an individual or entity has not looked at or purchased a business before does not mean he or she will not purchase yours. Every buyer or aggregator has to begin somewhere, or may have a specific need that your business can satisfy.

Although suitors who have never purchased a business before have no track record, their general business methods may tell you a great deal about how the proceedings might go. Therefore, spend time assessing how they conduct their own business. Day-to-day behavior can provide a good indication of conduct during and after the sale. In particular, focus on how the buyer acts when speaking with your staff, at meetings, and when dealing with others, including his or her own staff and advisors.

Items to Consider

Regardless of whether this is the buyer's first purchase or fiftieth, plan on doing your own research, or due diligence. Here is a list of some of the questions you should try to answer:

- Is the potential buyer genuinely interested in acquiring the business, or might it be merely on an exploratory mission to obtain information about your operations?

- What do the buyer and its business do?

- What is the buyer's reputation?

- If the buyer has made any prior acquisitions, how were these businesses operated after the purchase?

- Does the buyer have sufficient real financial resources to make the acquisition? Are these resources dependent on others?

- Is the buyer committed to making the acquisition? Why do you believe this?

- Will the buyers want your employees to remain after the sale?

- Do you think your employees will want to work for the buyer?

- Do you think your existing customers will be comfortable with the buyer purchasing the business?

- Will your customers remain with the business after the sale?

- Will the buyer allow your existing culture to remain after the acquisition?

- Will the buyer operate the business in a manner that will enable it to prosper?

- Has the buyer been regularly involved in litigation?

- Are the buyer's credit reports and financial statements in good order? If not, what are the reasons?

In sum, you and your advisors should assess the buyer just as the buyer is assessing you. Trust your gut feelings, but continually and discreetly solicit input from advisors and other people you respect—including, whenever possible, some who have observed and interacted with the buyer on a frequent basis.

Having even general answers to these questions will help to allay undue fears about a buyer's integrity and intentions. You always should run a search on the buyer and his or her company or companies on Google, Yahoo, MSN, and other search engines and review their credit reports via Dun & Bradstreet and similar credit reporting agencies. If the buyer company is publicly held, review all Securities and Exchange Commission filings and any analysts' reports on the business as well as any other relevant information.

Being Too Cautious

Although it is healthy to be circumspect about buyers, many business owners are too cautious about disclosing information. Extreme reluctance will
severely impede a prospective deal: Buyers who perceive that they are encountering resistance (whether it is actual or not) may choose to focus their
attention and resources on other endeavors.

Remember that much of the information potential buyers seek about
you is probably already available through a variety of sources, including
other businesses, trade groups, customers, suppliers, and via the Internet
and credit reporting services.

QUICK TIP: VIEW YOUR CREDIT REPORT

*Monitor and review your files with credit reporting agencies annually to ascer-
tain if they are accurate. Request that any inaccuracies or errors be corrected.*

For example, many IT companies provide financial statements to their
suppliers and customers, who in turn may disseminate the data to others. If
your suppliers or customers are government entities, public agencies, or reg-
ulated businesses, the data may be in the public domain already. A knowledgeable and determined outsider (including a competitor) may be able to
use public sources to obtain much of what you are trying to protect. In
many cases, an astute competitor may have the data already. Balance your
concern over disclosure with the understanding that information on your
company is probably not as confidential and difficult to obtain as you
thought and may be in the hands of competitors already.

Top Concerns

Companies typically are most concerned about disclosing this information:

- Financial data, including sales, margins, and operating costs
- Employee names, telephone numbers, titles, job descriptions, and
  compensation
- Customers, including contact people, pricing, and special needs your
  company satisfies
- Suppliers, including contacts, level of business, and pricing

- Proprietary technical information, including code, documentation, bug reports, and support statistics

Financial Data

During the initial phase of the buyer's due diligence, you should consider presenting only summary financial data; however, if much of this information is already in the public domain or can be easily compiled and reconstructed, you should be less concerned about this and you may choose to present more detailed data.

Employee Information

This will be a vexing area for you. In many IT firms, employees are the single most important and valuable asset—and potentially the most transient one. It is important that, before you release any information about your company, the buyer agrees in the Confidentiality Agreement, which will be discussed in the next Chapter, that he or she cannot and will not solicit or hire your employees for a significant period of time. However, an astute and honorable potential buyer will rightly question what happens if an existing employee of your business applies for a position at the buyer's company at some time in the near future. Where feasible, hiring this employee should be prohibited due to the agreement. However, this prohibition may be unenforceable in some jurisdictions.

However, if you are selling your business to a large regional, national, or international company with multiple offices, some of which can be located throughout the country or world, it is entirely possible that one of your employees might apply for a job at one of the acquiring company's offices. For that company to advise its local managers not to hire anyone from your business would be unfeasible, and it would draw attention to your business.

You may want to consider not providing employee contact information and have the confidentiality agreement prohibit the potential suitor from contacting your employees without your approval.

Customers

Although it is common for a potential buyer to know the names of your major customers, your pricing structure, and when the contracts with your customers expire, the acquisition process provides an opportunity to not only confirm their names but also to learn more about the individual customers, develop relationships with them, and learn more about your sales and marketing strategies. Naturally, if the acquisition falls through, the potential buyer can then solicit your customers. If your customers have high switching costs or are extremely loyal, this is not a major concern, but if their switching costs are low or if your business is in an industry where customers periodically change IT suppliers, this concern should be addressed in the confidentiality agreement.

One common solution may be for you to identify customers without using their names but merely by a code letter or number (A, B, C; 1, 2, 3), with the names revealed after closing. The purchaser would have recourse against you if the data provided were inaccurate. Another compromise is to provide the customer information to a third party under an agreement stating that the information will not be divulged except to the buyer after the sale. But remember, if the suitor is one of your competitors, it probably will already know the identities and other relevant details of your largest customers and, possibly, many if not all of your customers.

However, even these solutions may not fully resolve the matter. Many times a buyer wants to meet with key customers. If that is the case and there is no alternative, you might want to propose that the buyer agree to interview only a limited number.

At all times, both buyer and seller must attempt to balance the interests and legitimate requests and concerns of all parties in the proposed sale.

Another compromise to surmount this impasse or stalemate may be via a customer satisfaction survey, which is a tool used regularly by many companies in the ordinary course of business. This can be an excellent way for a potential buyer to gauge customer satisfaction and dissatisfaction without divulging that your business is for sale. A survey can also be used to permit a potential buyer, properly monitored, to contact customers to learn more about their relationship with your business. Or an independent survey firm can be retained for this purpose.

Suppliers

Just as you are concerned about releasing customer names and contact information, so should you be concerned about providing the names and pricing structures of key suppliers. For example, if one of your several suppliers is contemplating purchasing your business, you would be leery of providing information on other suppliers' pricing or your level of dependence on them. In addition, some of your relationships with other suppliers may change (or evaporate) if a supplier purchases your business. Even the leak of a contemplated sale can put severe strain on supplier and possibly customer relationships. Moreover, an ultimate decision not to sell to a supplier to whom you contemplated a sale and furnished information can have a negative effect on your future relationship.

One way to allay these concerns is to provide supplier-related information in stages. Doing this has the disadvantage of making the process longer and more arduous, reducing the likelihood of the sale, because many buyers look at several potential targets and would naturally gravitate to the one where less resistance is encountered and the process less onerous and cumbersome. However, an astute buyer will gravitate to the business that makes the most economic sense as an acquisition even if the process is protracted.

If despite these alternatives, you are still concerned about loosing existing customers to a potential suitor in the event the sale is not consummated, your Confidential Agreement should prohibit the suitor from soliciting your customers for a period of time.

Proprietary Technical Information

The release of proprietary technical information to someone who does not ultimately purchase the business can be very damaging. In many instances, the buyer may not need this information before the sale. It may suffice if the buyer's senior technical people simply speak to their counterparts at your firm. If you are persuaded that the buyer really needs to see source code and documentation, and you are still reluctant to release it, one compromise might be to retain an independent third party to evaluate the data and provide a very general report to the buyer, without detail.

CHAPTER 14

Confidentiality: Limiting Data Dissemination and Preparing Confidentiality Agreements

In the last chapter, we examined the need for confidentiality when competitors are potential buyers, how to evaluate buyers, and related matters. The focus of this chapter is on how to limit the use and dissemination of data and prepare a confidentiality agreement. In addition, we take a practical look at how to keep the negotiation process confidential.

LIMITING THE DISSEMINATION OF DATA

Although you should be very hesitant about releasing information until the buyer's motives are confirmed, a parallel aim should be to limit the number of people involved in the process on both sides. In particular, information should be released only to a limited number of the buyer's representatives, and in a controlled fashion.

As the sale process progresses, several key procedures can minimize the risk of information falling into the wrong hands. They include:

- Exercising caution in all communications
- Conducting as much of the due diligence as possible outside your facility. For instance, you should:
  - Hold as many of the meetings as possible off-site in locations such as a hotel room, attorney's, C.P.A.'s or other professional's office, and airport frequent flyer club.

- Use your firm's outside advisors to field questions, when feasible.

- Provide the acquirer with secure telephone, fax numbers, and e-mail address where you and other key employees can be reached to avoid going through company networks, switchboards, and servers.

- Place a dedicated fax line and machine in your office or home to avoid confidential incoming documents' being seen by others. Another alternative is to utilize a computer fax service where the faxes are routed directly to your computer.

But even when these steps are taken, many of the people with knowledge of the contemplated transaction will be outside of your control. These parties include the potential acquirer's employees, advisors, accountants, bankers, and attorneys. You should discuss your concerns and ways to avoid problems with potential buyers at the outset. At a minimum, everyone involved in the potential transaction should have its strict confidential nature emphasized to them, and the steps being taken to avoid disclosure should be detailed. Whenever an infraction or potential infraction is discovered, appropriate steps should be taken, including speaking with all individuals involved, devising procedures to avoid future infractions, and insisting that similar problems not recur. If possible, it may also be helpful to speak with the unintended recipients of the information, if you can do that smoothly.

It is also important to recognize that as the sale progresses, many astute employees will notice that you, along with your key employees, are frequently out of the office, in closed-door meetings, or involved in long telephone conversations. Consider in advance how you will address questions on this when they are posed.

THE CONFIDENTIALITY AGREEMENT

One way for any business to protect its information while being sold is to require all potential buyers to sign a confidentiality or nondisclosure agreement. These agreements frequently are referred to as CAs or NDAs. Such an agreement typically provides that the party whose information is wrongfully used or disseminated can obtain injunctive relief—as well as monetary damages—through the courts.

A note of caution: The confidentiality agreement is a powerful weapon for you, but only if the potential buyer has integrity, the wherewithal to monitor compliance, and the financial resources to pay damages. Remember, any representation is only as good as the person or entity providing it. This is especially true if the suitor has a practice, code of conduct, and culture that prohibits ethical violations. The potential buyer who agrees to be subject to monetary damages but has no assets may be making an empty promise. This promise becomes even more hollow if the buyer realizes he or she may have nothing to lose by disclosing confidential information. Conversely, if the potential buyer has financial resources far in excess of your company's, litigating an infraction may be extremely expensive for you. Always keep in mind that a competitor or potential competitor may be disingenuous, posing as a buyer, and may go through a large part of the buying process with the sole intent of obtaining intelligence on your business. Moreover, often it is difficult to prove that the agreement has been violated and to quantify the damages.

Buyers and sellers always should retain legal counsel to prepare and review all confidentiality agreements and any other documents connected with the purchase and sale. Having an experienced lawyer prepare and review these documents will help ensure that your business receives the fullest protection possible. The value of this protection will more than justify both the time and expense. However, it is important to impress upon your attorney the need for a prompt response to your requests and questions.

Some of the points a confidentiality agreement should address include:

- Names of the parties to the agreement
- Who can receive the confidential data
- Definition of confidential information
- Exceptions
- Time period
- Provision to return data upon termination
- Agreement not to hire the other's employees or solicit customers.
- Governing law
- Damages

Names of the Parties to the Agreement

Typically the parties to the agreement include the buying and selling companies as well as the people who will be involved in the transaction. An individual with the authority to bind each organization, typically a senior corporate officer, should execute the agreement.

Who Can Receive the Confidential Data

It is common for these agreements to provide that either party can share information with its attorneys, accountants, employees, and other advisors or professionals, so long as these parties agree to maintain the confidentiality of the data under the same or more restrictive terms.

As a precaution, the agreement can limit the number of individuals in either organization to whom the buyer can speak concerning the transaction. This will reduce the disclosure of confidential information to unauthorized personnel. The list can be expanded as the transaction progresses.

QUICK TIP: LIMIT USE AND DISSEMINATION OF DATA

If one of your competitors is a potential acquirer, you probably will not want your data to be provided to their sales, marketing, and product development people.

As an aside, when preparing for the sale and the buyer's due diligence, first you should compile a list of people in your organization who definitely will need to know about it and with whom a prudent buyer may want to speak as the negotiations progress. The acquirers probably will need to speak with them at some point anyway, since they will be in a position to learn of meetings, requests, or other events that are out of the ordinary. Although the list will grow as the transaction progresses, the initial group typically will include your chief financial officer, controller or bookkeeper, plus a few trusted colleagues and assistants. As the process continues, the acquirer may ask to speak with senior members of the your management team; these individuals might include your chief technology officer, chief information officer, and vice presidents for sales and development.

It is best for this list to be expanded only when necessary. As each new person is advised of the potential transaction, he or she should be informed of the need for confidentiality and be told who else has been informed of the pending deal.

Definition of Confidential Information

The agreement should clearly state what information is confidential. Some agreements use a broad definition, including all information provided, while others limit the scope. Some agreements stipulate that for information to be deemed confidential, it must be marked or stamped accordingly. However, this requirement does not cover information transmitted orally, obtained in meetings, or during observation of the business, and places an onerous burden on the seller to stamp or mark every page of every document that is faxed, mailed, emailed, hand-delivered, and/or given to the buyer and his or her representatives. Such information needs to be protected through other stipulations, or the agreement must require the disclosing party to follow up oral disclosures immediately in writing, which can also be onerous.

Exceptions

It is also important to define what information is excluded from the confidentiality agreement. Exclusions typically include information that is:

- Already known by the recipient without any breach or violation of any law or confidentiality agreement
- Developed independently
- Already in the public domain, through no violation of any agreement
- Required to be provided by subpoena or other government or legal processes

In this last situation, it is typical that the party receiving a subpoena or other government demand for information be required to inform the other party immediately, to afford that party the opportunity to quash the request. It seems equitable that the receiving party should not have to incur any costs to quash the subpoena if the releasing party is the one who is attempting to block the release.

Time Period

The agreement also should provide for a period in the future during which the receiving party cannot make use of any of the data obtained in connection with a failed transaction. Every industry and business has its own guidelines for some, three to five years is sufficient as most, if not all, of the data provided becomes stale before then anyway, others require far longer periods. All parties should be reasonable in this regard.

Provision to Return Data upon Termination

To inject a sense of urgency and finality into the proposed transaction, confidentiality agreements frequently stipulate a deadline after which the recipient of the confidential data has to return the information to the provider if the transaction has not been consummated or mutually terminated. Both parties can agree to extend the deadline if the transaction is still proceeding and progressing as it nears. To eliminate inconvenience and suspicion, especially when documents are transmitted electronically (meaning as a copy), NDA's typically allow an officer of one party to provide a statement to the other certifying that the data have indeed been destroyed. It is important that before the person provides such a representation, a thorough review is made to ascertain that the copies, whether they are in electronic or paper form, are in fact destroyed.

Agreement Not to Hire the Other's Employees or Solicit Customers

Confidentiality agreements frequently provide that the potential buyer cannot hire or solicit the potential seller's employees for a specified period of time. This provision should be considered carefully. Many large companies insist that a "no solicit" provision replace any "no hire" provision in the agreement: The buyer cannot solicit your employees, but your employees can apply for jobs. If you wish to try to stick with "solicit," be alert to how the clause is written. For example, would solicitation include placing a large and general help-wanted advertisement in the hometown newspaper of the your business? (Of course, an unscrupulous buyer seeking to steal key employees can subvert this prohibition by advising them to indicate that they sought employment on their own or respond to an upcoming newspaper advertisement.)

A similar prohibition can be placed on the potential buyer not soliciting the seller's customers for a specified period of time.

Governing Law

The agreement should specify which jurisdiction's laws apply and in what jurisdiction any claim or dispute must be filed. Although this becomes an issue only in the event of a breach or alleged breach, neither party wants to incur the inconvenience of litigating as well as the cost of traveling to the other business's home state, even if local counsel are obtained, to defend its actions or to sue.

Damages

Some confidentiality agreements include a provision that outlines the scope of potential liquidated damages; others do not. *Liquidated damages* refer to an estimated amount the parties agree to, to be paid upon a breach by either side. Arriving at an estimate or a method to calculate the damages is not always possible or feasible.

It is extremely difficult to calculate the damages a business will incur if the potential buyer discloses confidential information; in certain instances, the disclosure of customer names, pricing and sales data can be devastating. As a result, these agreements frequently provide that damages cannot be easily calculated and a trial may be required, in extreme circumstances, to determine the extent and amount. Moreover, such agreements usually provide for injunctive relief in the event of a breach, including court issuance of a restraining or cease-and-desist order to stop immediate and irreparable harm to the business.

PRACTICAL STEPS

When preparing for a sale, several steps should be taken to help maintain confidentiality:

- Everyone involved should be instructed where to send all correspondence via mail, fax, or e-mail. They should be advised to take appropriate safeguards so their offices do not send correspondence to or telephone inappropriate individuals or addresses at the business.

- Mail should be sent off-site to a secure address where it will not be opened and viewed by unintended individuals. Even if your employees do not open executive mail, they may be alarmed if you start receiving a lot of mail in the office marked "Confidential" or "To Be Opened Only by Addressee."

- E-mail should be sent to a secure address where it will not be inadvertently viewed by anyone unaware of the pending sale.

- Your attorneys, accountants, and other advisors—as well as outsiders familiar with the proposed transaction—must know which people are knowledgeable about the intended transaction and should be advised to limit their communications to them.

Notify all advisors who will be submitting itemized invoices to review and edit them closely beforehand to avoid inadvertently disclosing confidential information to your accounting or financial support employees. Secretaries, bookkeepers, and file clerks at your company may handle such statements all the time, and a detailed invoice from your business's attorney, Certified Public Accountant, or business advisors could indicate telephone conversations, meetings, or hourly work performed in connection with the impending sale. Similar cautions should heeded by you, as well as by your own employees, who may submit expense reimbursement requests in connection with such sale-related activities as trips or meals. This becomes an issue if you and other employees make numerous unexplained trips to the location of a potential buyer. Employees who review expense reports may be able to surmise that a transaction is pending.

Or, instead of editing their submissions, advisors can submit invoices directly to an individual at the business who is familiar with the possible impending transaction.

QUICK TIP: REMEMBER YOUR EMPLOYEES ARE ASTUTE

Remember that most of your employees are observant and/or astute. They will notice when you and colleagues are involved in more meetings than usual with outsiders who are not introduced to them. Advise outsiders visiting your offices to be sensitive to your dress code. If employees normally dress casually, outsiders will be conspicuous if they arrive in designer suits and expensive shoes. Similarly, if it is standard procedure for visitors to register with a receptionist, ask your buyer and his or her colleagues to do so and to be discreet when listing their employer, names, purpose of visit, and so on.

Notwithstanding these safeguards, precautionary measures sometimes fail in small, centralized IT businesses. It therefore may be more efficient to have a meeting with all employees early in the process to disclose the possible sale. Doing this will help allay concerns, and many employees will appreciate your candor and be less anxious about the possible change. Moreover, if some key employees are scheduled to receive bonuses at the time of sale, they will want to try to assist in the transaction. If you do advise employees of a pending transaction, it is important to inform them, on an ongoing basis, of the likelihood that the deal will be consummated and the projected time frame to the closing.

A sample confidentiality agreement is shown in Exhibit 14.1.

EXHIBIT 14.1   SAMPLE CONFIDENTIALITY AGREEMENT

CONFIDENTIALITY AGREEMENT

Re: Confidential Information

Dear XXXXXX:

This letter shall set forth our mutual understandings with respect to Confidential Information received by XXXXXXXXXXXX (Buyer), its officers, directors, stockholders, employees, agents and affiliates (collectively, "You") from YYYYYYY, its employees or agents ("Seller") in connection with a possible acquisition of the assets or stock of Seller by You (the "Transaction"). The term "Confidential Information" shall mean nonpublic, confidential or proprietary technical, engineering, financial, environmental, economic, legal, regulatory, commercial, and business information data, records, and material furnished by Seller (irrespective of the form of communication) to You or which becomes available to You in writing, by drawings, by inspection of Seller's facilities or in any other way.

Confidential Information shall not include:
(a) information that is in Your possession at the time of disclosure and not subject to any agreement of confidentiality;
(b) information that is now or hereafter becomes part of the public knowledge or literature through no action of You; or
(c) information that is hereafter received by You from a third party without any agreement of confidentiality. Confidential Information shall not be deemed to be within the foregoing exceptions merely because such information is embraced by more general information within any such exception.

(Continues)

EXHIBIT 14.1   CONTINUED

XXXXXXX
DATE
Page 2

You recognize that in order to induce Seller to disclose Confidential Information, nei-ther You, nor Your representatives will, except as required by law, communicate, dis-close, divulge, or make use of any Confidential Information without Seller's prior written agreement.

Except as otherwise permitted herein, for a period beginning on the date hereof and ending _____ years from the date this Transaction terminates, You agree not to disclose any Confidential Information received hereunder or use any Confidential Infor-mation except in connection with your evaluation of the possible acquisition of Seller. You shall protect such confidential information with the same degree of care as you use to protect your own confidential information. You may disclose the Confidential Information to Your advisors and consultants, provided that You first obtain agree-ment by such recipients to restrictions on the disclosure and use of the Confidential Information which are at least as restrictive as those which You have accepted under this Agreement.

You expressly agree that you shall not discuss this transaction with any employees or agents of Seller, except for such persons that I provide to you in writing. At this time you should limit your communications to _____, _____ and _____.

In the event Confidential Information is sought from You or Your representatives by any court (in a litigation) or legislative or administrative body (by oral questions, or interrogatories, subpoena, civil investigations, demand or similar process), You agree to:

(a) resist disclosure of said Confidential Information on the grounds that You are under an obligation not to disclose Confidential Information to third parties;

(b) promptly notify Seller of the attempt to compel the disclosure of Confidential Information in order to afford Seller an opportunity to assist You in Your efforts to resist disclosure or to seek an appropriate protective order on its own; and

(c) assist Seller in seeking a protective order to preserve the Confidential nature of the Confidential Information.

If a definitive agreement concerning the Transaction is not executed within forty-five (45) days of the date hereof, or if negotiations cease before then, You shall, at the written request of Seller, return to Seller all originals and photocopies of

EXHIBIT 14.1 CONTINUED

XXXXXXXXXXXX
DATE
Page 3

documents (in whatever form) containing Confidential Information; provided that, in lieu of delivering such portion that includes derivative products (work papers) to Seller, You shall deliver Your certificate (certified by a corporate officer) to Seller certifying that the obligation to return and destroy documents has been fully performed.

You acknowledge that You shall obtain no rights in any of the Confidential Information other than as expressly set forth herein. You agree that should the Transaction not occur, for a period of _____ years from the date hereof you shall not 1) hire any current or future employee of Seller or 2) solicit any customer or client of the Seller.

You expressly agree that Seller, in addition to any other rights or remedies that Seller may possess, shall be entitled to injunctive and other equitable relief to prevent breach of this Agreement by You, and Seller shall be entitled to reasonable attorneys fees and expenses in association with the enforcement of this Agreement.

If any of the terms set forth in this Agreement, or any part thereof, should, for any reason whatsoever, be declared invalid by a court of competent jurisdiction, the validity or enforceability of the remainder of such terms shall not thereby be adversely effected.

This Agreement shall be binding upon and inure to the benefit of You, Seller as well as Seller's and Your respective successors and assigns.

This Agreement shall be governed by and interpreted in accordance with the internal laws of the State of _____ (without regard to conflict of laws principles). Any claim or dispute hereunder shall be resolved exclusively in the State or Federal Courts sitting in the State of _____. This is the complete agreement between the parties and may only be modified by a writing signed by the party to be bound.

No binding representation shall be made or implied by virtue of disclosure of Confidential Information. Any binding representation or agreement with respect to the Transaction, shall only be contained in definitive documentation signed by the parties to this agreement. Each party reserves the right to terminate the negotiations at any time.

As you know I am the Seller's _____, and I am sending you this letter in that capacity.

If the above meets with your approval, kindly sign a copy of this letter and return it to me.

Very truly yours,

_____

Seller

(Continues)

EXHIBIT 14.1   CONTINUED

XXXXXXXXXXX
DATE
Page 4

AGREED TO AND ACCEPTED:
By: _____
Name_____
Title_____
DATE _____

RJC:rs
Enclosures

confagre/wharton

CHAPTER 15

Letter of Intent

$\mathbf{A}$s the acquisition process for an information technology firm proceeds and becomes more serious, eventually the terms of the proposed transaction must be formalized. When the potential buyer has performed an initial analysis of the target company and decides to move forward, the next step for both parties is to sign a letter of intent, which is frequently referred to as an LOI.

Prior to the LOI being issued, the buyer probably will have met with and discussed the business with the seller and may have reviewed these five items, which will have enticed the buyer to proceed toward a possible purchase:

1. The selling "memo" or "book"
2. Financial information on the business including financial statements, year-to-date results, limited management reports, and possibly tax returns
3. The business's organizational structure
4. Marketing material
5. Information obtained from the business's Web site and external sources

Up to this point, the terms of the transaction may or may not have been discussed orally, and frequently, no written offers may have been made. The purpose of the LOI is to formalize the proposed transaction terms. It may be signed before, during, or after the due diligence period, when the buyer determines the validity of the seller's account of the business. However the buyer may prefer that this be executed sooner, rather than later, in the process.

The letter of intent lays out the framework of the proposed deal. Prior to drafting an LOI, the buyer may submit a "term sheet" that specifies the salient components of the transaction that eventually will be embodied in the letter of intent. This term sheet need not be signed by either party; it serves simply to establish the sale framework for all parties. However, it is not necessary, but it is frequently helpful to have a letter of intent. In some instances, the parties can agree to skip this step and execute a contract.

Assuming a letter of intent is submitted, it generally will cover these components of the proposed deal in more detail than the term sheet:

- Transaction structure.
- Any special accounting or tax considerations.
- Assets to be acquired and liabilities assumed.
- Purchase price.
- Terms of the notes or stock to be conveyed.
- Estimated closing date.
- Conditions for consummating the transaction. These may include completion of due diligence, the execution or signing of an acquisition agreement, and the receipt of any needed government or regulatory approvals.
- Any circumstances under which the parties are no longer obligated to complete the transaction.
- A requirement for exclusivity, which requires that the seller not speak with any other potential buyers of the business except with the prior knowledge and consent of the buyer. This may also be referred to as a "no-shop" or "stand-down" clause.
- Any breakup fees or costs, if any, for which the parties are liable.
- A requirement that the seller continue to operate the business in the normal and ordinary course and obtain the buyer's approval for any extraordinary actions.
- Any other conditions or requirements of the sale.

There can be many contingencies in a letter of intent. The seller can require a nonrefundable deposit, but this is rare. In most cases, the LOI requires that the terms of the transaction remain confidential.

Most of the provisions of the LOI are typically non-binding except of the terms dealing with confidentiality and exclusivity. However, the parties may agree that other provisions are binding.

The letter of intent typically provides an outside date by which the closing must occur, and it can indicate reasons why the deal cannot be consummated. A common reason for allowing the deal to be terminated is the buyer's dissatisfaction with information obtained during the due diligence period, either from the company or from outside sources. However, from the seller's view, this provision should be based on a discernible standard. The letter of intent can also cover, in a very broad sense, the terms of the employment contracts for the current owner(s). In the sale of IT companies, it is very common for a buyer to require current owners (assuming you are active in the business) as well as key managers to sign employment contracts with covenants not to compete for a specified period of time, which can range from a few months to several years. This can be beneficial to everyone in several ways. First, it allows (indeed, gives incentive to) current owners and managers to assist in the business's transition, which will decrease concern among employees, customers, and suppliers when the sale is announced. Second, it can provide for an easier transition out of the business for you. Conversely, if you are unable to continue to work due to sickness (or death), this will typically reduce the price the purchaser will pay. If the compensation that you will be receiving is significant, you should consider purchasing life and disability insurance to enable you and/or your estate to be indemnified in the event of death or disability.

A copy of a sample letter of intent is shown in Exhibit 15.1.

EXHIBIT 15.1   SAMPLE LETTER OF INTENT

Selling Associates
Philadelphia, PA

Attention of Paul G.

Re: Letter of Intent
Asset Purchase from Selling Associates, Inc.

Dear Mr. G.:

This is a letter of intent setting forth our mutual understandings concerning the terms and conditions by which The Chalfin Group Inc., a New Jersey corporation ("Chalfin")will purchase all of the assets (except as set forth in paragraph 3 hereof) of Selling Associates, Inc., a Pennsylvania corporation ("Seller"). We do not intend that a legally binding commitment with respect to the proposed transaction will be created by your acceptance of these terms; however, by endorsing its approval on the copy of this letter, Chalfin and Seller agree that the provisions below relating to exclusivity and confidentiality (see paragraphs 13 and 14, respectively) shall be fully binding on all parties.

1. The Purchaser shall either be Chalfin or an entity owned or controlled by Chalfin or its principal shareholders (hereinafter the "Purchaser").

2. Purchaser shall purchase upon the terms and conditions provided herein all the assets (collectively the "Assets") of Seller. The Assets shall include, without limitation:

    i.   All current salable, non-obsolete, non-damaged inventory;

    ii.   All supplies;

    iii.   All operating equipment including _____;

    iv.   The real estate associated with the business and all improvements thereon;

    v.   Accounts receivable;

    vi.   All goodwill of the business

    vi.   Other Assets ....; and

    vii.   All other assets of Seller, excluding the Excluded Assets.

3. The following Assets of the Seller (the "Excluded Assets") will be retained by Seller:

    i.   All cash and cash equivalents;

    ii.   All vehicles;

    iii   Life insurance policies; and

    iv.   Other Assets ....

4. Purchaser shall not assume any liability or debts of Seller of any kind, known or unknown except for the assumed liabilities including......

(Continues)

EXHIBIT 15.1   CONTINUED

5. The purchase price for the assets shall be $___ million payable as follows:

  i. By delivery of a Promissory Note of Purchaser (hereinafter referred to as the "Promissory Note") in the principal amount of $_____. The Promissory Note shall be [non-recourse] bearing interest at ___ percent. The Promissory Note shall be payable as follows: _____

_____

  ii. By cash, wire transfer, certified check, bank check, or attorney trust account check for $_____.

6. The purchase price for the Assets shall be adjusted dollar for dollar to the extent that the book value of the Assets at the closing are less than [$_____ or the book value of the Assets as provided on Seller's financial statements dated _____, 200_, which have been provided to the Purchaser (the "Financials")]. In this regard, the book value at the closing shall be determined consistently with the Financials, except that the accounts receivable shall be valued by _____. The book value of the Assets at closing shall not include any outstanding loans to shareholders, officers, and directors of the Seller, as well as the Excluded Assets.

7. The accounts receivable shall be guaranteed by Seller and its shareholders, and the principal amount of the Promissory Note shall be reduced by the amount of accounts receivable transferred at closing which have not been collected by Purchaser by the 180-day anniversary of the closing.

8. Employee 1, Employee 2 and Employee 3 shall be employed for a period of one year following the closing at the rate of _____ Thousand Dollars ($__,000.00), _____ Thousand Dollars ($__,000.00) and _____Thousand Dollars ($___,00.00), respectively. Thereafter, the Purchaser shall have the option of hiring these individuals on a commission or salary basis.

9. The Seller and each individual stockholder, Employee 1, Employee 2 and Employee 3, shall execute covenants against competition in a form satisfactory to the Purchaser.

10. The agreement to purchase the Assets shall be subject to the following conditions:

  i. The receipt of a loan commitment for $ _____, for a term of ____ years at an interest rate of ___%.

  ii. The Purchaser being satisfied with a review, examination, and verification of the Assets and the earning capacity of the business;

  iii. The Purchaser being satisfied with a review and examination of Purchaser's books and records (including contracts);

  iv. Seller providing Purchaser with all appropriate governmental or necessary approvals with respect to this transfer and the operation of the facility;

  v. Title to the real estate shall be marketable and insuring at regular rates without material exception by title company of Purchaser's selection; and

  vi. Other commitments............

EXHIBIT 15.1 CONTINUED

11. The anticipated closing date is _____, 200_, or as soon as thereafter as is practical.

12. The Seller will continue to operate the business and maintain the property in its usual manner until the closing, and shall not make any substantial distribution of Assets, enter into any long-term contracts, or incur any extraordinary expenses without first consulting with the Purchaser.

13. The Seller shall supply any materials and documents that shall be reasonably requested by Purchaser or its representatives, within ten (10) days of any request. For forty-five (45) days from the signing of this letter of intent, the Seller (or any representative of or for the Seller) shall not negotiate with anyone other than Purchaser for the sale of its business, Assets, or stock.

14. Both parties agree that without the consent of the other, it shall not reveal any information it has received concerning the other party to third parties (other than professional advisors). No announcement of this letter of intent, disclosure of the transactions contemplated hereby, or disclosure of the terms and conditions of this proposed transaction shall be made without the mutual written consent of Seller and Chalfin.

15. Each party to the transaction shall be responsible for and pay its own costs and expenses.

16. This letter agreement is not intended to be a legally-binding commitment with respect to the proposed transaction. A legally-binding commitment will only result from the execution and delivery of definitive purchase agreements. However, by accepting this letter agreement, the provisions in paragraphs 13 and 14, relating to exclusivity and confidentiality, respectively, shall be fully binding on all parties.

17. This letter supersedes all prior correspondence and verbal discussions between Chalfin and Seller. If you are in agreement with the terms outlined above, please indicate by signing where indicated below on the enclosed copy of this letter and returning it to us no later than _____, 200_.

Very truly yours,

THE CHALFIN GROUP INC.

BY:_____
Name:
Title:

RJC:rs
Enclosure

ACCEPTED AND AGREED:
Selling Associates Inc.

BY:_____
NAME: Date:
Title:

CHAPTER 16

Due Diligence

After you and the acquiring party have reached an understanding about the purchase of your information technology business, the buyer must assemble and then verify critical information about your company.

The due diligence process is an essential part of the purchase. Due diligence typically includes gathering information on your company's business processes, its financial health, and its customer base, among many other factors. Due diligence enables the acquirer to quantify the risks he or she is assuming as well as the potential benefits that will be obtained. Since all IT businesses assume ongoing risks every day, no-risk deals are impossible. However, a buyer can reduce risk significantly by attempting to learn the details of potential problems and opportunities your business offers.

It is important for the seller to remember that while the buyer is assessing the business's risks, it is also analyzing the positive attributes such as cost savings, overall revenue enhancements, management and organizational depth and future opportunities. The potential risks need to be continually balanced against the benefits the business will provide. Ideally, you should be prepared for information requests at any time. You will gain a tremendous competitive advantage if most of that information is complete, well documented, and readily accessible.

Although due diligence serves the interests of the buyer, you should understand the process and must cooperate in it to achieve your own goal. Inaccurate or incomplete disclosure can delay the purchase, reduce the price you get, create liability after the sale, or cancel the sale altogether. Prudent sellers regard due diligence as a necessary evil; it is an invasive and burdensome process.

To prepare, you and your entire management team should carefully review, analyze, and prepare—beforehand—a list of the information any buyer will likely request, along with potential questions, issues, and concerns. This list should be reviewed with your business attorney, certified public accountant, and other trusted outsiders and advisors who can objectively review the information and suggest questions that probably will come up.

Because each buyer has concerns and reasons for purchasing a business, each due diligence process is unique and has its own requests and demands. Some of the common questions, many of which overlap, that an acquirer will want answered during the process may include:

- Does your company operate ethically, honestly, and with integrity?
- Have there been any fundamental changes in the markets the company operates in that will change the underlying business model? Have these changes been considered in the projections?
- What is special about your company?
- What solutions does the company offer?
- Do the solutions work? Do they need to be updated? If yes, what will be the cost?
- What is the projected demand for the company's current and future offerings?
- How can the solutions be integrated with the buyer's offerings and marketed to its customers?
- Who are the company's current and potential competitors?
- Who are the company's current and potential customers?
- What portion of your sales is concentrated among your five largest customers? How many of the largest customers account for 10 percent and 20 percent of your annual sales? Do these customers change or evolve each year?
- Who are your company's current and potential suppliers?
- What is the status of plans to develop new products or services?
- What are the business's long-term plans?
- What additional resources (if any) does your company need to achieve its near-term and long-term goals?
- What are the impediments to your company's growth? This can include capital, trained employees, and competition.

- What are the performance metrics of the industry your company operates in?
- How does your company's performance compare with industry averages and leaders?
- What can be done to improve performance?
- What are the projections for the next few years? Does your company have a history of meeting or exceeding projections?
- How can or will your business's employees, salaries, IT systems, offerings, and overall operating environment be integrated into the buyer's business, or how can the buyer's business be integrated into your business to achieve the greatest synergies?

Apart from these somewhat general questions, acquirers will have their own checklist, which will cover many of the same fundamental points. The appendix to this chapter contains many of the kinds of concerns buyers may have. Reviewing this list as early as possible will help you collect the information that may be requested and anticipate possible questions. (Comments on the information requests are italicized.)

Whenever conducting the due diligence process, it is important that both the buyer and seller be aware of the potential cost versus benefit of this work. Certainly no one wants to spend hours upon hours of time attempting to verify relatively insignificant items. Although there are benefits to both sides in being thorough and complete, diminishing returns are quickly approached. Just as buyers should be mindful if requests are onerous and irrelevant, so you the seller should be mindful that delays in providing the information will be unsettling.

Both the buyer and seller should approach this process with an open mind. The seller should understand that the due diligence process will require the attention and energy of many people in its organization. The buyer should understand that in many closely held businesses, not all of the requested records, reports, and analyses might be available. When this occurs, the buyer and seller should try to resolve these issues.

It is also important that you, the seller, keep a copy of every document that is provided to the buyer. In addition, every submission to the buyer should include a transmission letter enumerating the information that is being provided. Typically the seller's attorney, intermediary, and CPA will request a copy of every submission in case questions arise in the future, either before or after the sale.

Due Diligence Checklist

A. Organization and Capitalization

1a. List the names of the business and its subsidiaries, as well as any fictitious names used by the business and its subsidiaries.

> **QUICK TIP**
>
> *At the outset, the buyer wants to determine whether your business is legally organized and in compliance with all applicable laws and regulations.*

1b. Assemble articles or certificates of incorporation and bylaws for the company and each of its subsidiaries, including amendments. If the businesses are organized as LLCs, furnish copies of the certificates of formation. If the businesses are organized as partnerships, obtain copies of the partnership agreements.

2a. List all jurisdictions in which the company does business or owns property. *The definition of doing business can be broad. This list will assist in determining where the new business should file tax returns, register with state and local authorities, and so on.*

2b. Review certificate of good standing and certificates with tax status for all jurisdictions in which the company does business.

3. Assemble minutes of board of directors' and shareholders' meetings of the company and its subsidiaries for the past five years, including minutes of any committees of the boards of directors.

> **QUICK TIP**
>
> *Because minutes tell the story of the business at a very high level, it is important to maintain them. If there were no formal meetings or minutes, don't attempt to create them and/or backdate documents; instead, hold a meeting in which all prior acts performed by the business are affirmed and ratified. Doing this may involve listing your business's major events and decisions.*

4a. Prepare a description of all classes of capital stock, convertible securities, warrants, and options of the company.

> **QUICK TIP**
>
> *Sometimes companies grant to their large clients options or rights of first refusal to buy all or part of the business. If this has occurred, appropriate releases or waivers must be executed by these option holders.*

4b. List the names, addresses, and holdings of all beneficial owners of the company's equity securities as well as warrants and options and their respective exercise price(s). Review and reconcile stock ledger; treasury stock; issued and unissued stock.

5a. Review all stockholders', buy-sell, cross-purchase, operating, partnership, and joint-venture agreements. These documents often can limit the transferability of company stock. Waivers or releases may be needed from the appropriate individuals or entities.

5b. Review all trust agreements, as well as voting trusts, outstanding proxies, or other restrictions on transferability and/or voting of the company's securities, and any amendments.

5c. Determine the existence and nature of any preemptive rights.

> **QUICK TIP**
>
> *The documents specified in 5a, b, and c often can limit the transferability of company stock. Waivers or releases may be needed from the appropriate individuals or entities.*

5d. Provide copies of any investment or subscription agreements with current or potential investors outlining the business's and the investors' rights, responsibilities, and obligations.

6. Review all communications to shareholders (including annual and quarterly reports) by the company and any of its subsidiaries. *This includes transcripts, tapes, minutes, and summaries of the conference calls.*

7a. If not provided in response to a previous question, prepare a list of the current officers and directors of the company and its subsidiaries.

QUICK TIP

If the business has positions it intends to fill, indicate that intent. The same applies for any expected changes in the employee base, which can include pending offers of employment, resignation, and/or terminations.

7b. Prepare the company's current organizational chart.

QUICK TIP

In growing businesses, the organizational chart may have vacancies, which should be so indicated. This is understandable and expected.

8. Assemble all filings by the company with the Securities and Exchange Commission along with any other governmental regulatory agencies.

B. BUSINESS FINANCING

1. Obtain names and contact information for the lending officers for each bank and/or lender with which the company does business or has done business over the past five years.

2. Obtain copies of all credit, loan, and borrowing agreements and amendments.

3. Assemble all loan agreements, applications, mortgages, notes, guarantees, UCC-1's, indentures, and bonds.

QUICK TIP

Review these documents prior to due diligence to determine if they contain any information that must be addressed with potential buyers. Prior loan applications and resultant correspondence and documentation can provide substantial information about the business's history. A prudent buyer will review these documents carefully.

4. Collect all documents relating to all material sales and leasebacks of the business's real estate and capital equipment.

5. Collect all correspondence with lenders, including compliance reports.

QUICK TIP

You should already have apprised lending officers of the impending discussions and possibility of a sale; if not, do so as soon as possible since it is likely they will be contacted by the potential buyer.

C. LITIGATION AND CLAIMS

1. Collect and prepare a schedule of all pending or potential legal proceedings to which your company or its subsidiaries is a party. For each matter, provide a brief description of this information:
    *   Parties
    *   Nature of the proceeding
    *   Date commenced and method (remember that threats can be verbal)
    *   Damages or other relief sought
    *   Pleadings and correspondence with lawyer(s)

QUICK TIP

In today's litigious environment, many businesses are involved in lawsuits. Merely being a party to a suit does not render a business unsalable. However, you must provide full disclosure of the details of the lawsuit to the buyer.

---

2. Compile and review all applicable litigation insurance coverage.

3. Analyze and review all legal bills and statements.

QUICK TIP

A review of the business's legal invoices can provide an indication of any opportunities the business is pursuing and problems it has encountered.

---

4. Review all other correspondence with attorneys.

5. Review copies of all consent decrees, judgments, settlements, and other dispositions of legal proceedings to which the company has a continuing or contingent obligation of a material nature.

6. Obtain a list of all attorneys who are or have been retained by or on behalf of the company at any time over the past seven years. For each attorney:

   - Provide contact information.
   - Provide a summary of the work performed by the attorney for or on behalf of the company.
   - Provide copies of all invoices.
   - Speak with all attorneys to confirm the scope and status of all work performed.

QUICK TIP

The attorneys and other professionals will undoubtedly require that their client consent to them speaking with the purchaser.

D. RELEVANT REPORTS

1. Review all marketing materials prepared by your company and its competitors, suppliers, and customers.

QUICK TIP

A review of this information will help prepare for potential questions from the buyer.

2. Review competitors', suppliers', and industry Web sites.

QUICK TIP

An ongoing review of others' Web sites will help prepare you for potential questions from the buyer and provide you with information about the industry in which your business operates.

3. Analyze any industry product reviews or engineering reports on your company's offerings.

4. Review all customer surveys that relate to your company.

5. Review all consulting reports received as well as consultants' invoices, statements, and contracts.

E. INSURANCE COVERAGE AND CLAIMS

1. Review insurance policies and claims experience under all policies in which the business is the insured, owner, or beneficiary. This includes but is not limited to:

   - Property and casualty
   - Malpractice/errors and omissions
   - Automobile
   - Directors and officers
   - Workers' compensation
   - Health
   - Life
   - Disability
   - Employment practices

QUICK TIP

It is always important to review the scope and extent of your company's insurance coverage, to prevent any lapse of coverage during the sale process or at any other time.

---

2. For each policy listed in response to question E.1, provide:

   - Names of insurers
   - Names of insureds
   - Policy term
   - Premiums paid and due
   - Deductibles
   - Scope of coverage, conditions
   - Copies of all polices
   - Brokers
   - A listing of the claims experience for each policy

F. MANAGEMENT AND EMPLOYEE RELATIONS

1a.   Review compensation agreements and employment contracts for all officers, managers, employees, and members of the board of directors. This includes compensation plans for salespeople and outside sales representatives.

> **QUICK TIP**
>
> *In certain instances, either the buyer or the seller may want to buy out existing employment contracts or extend the contracts of certain key people. Frequently, employment contracts are in the form of letter agreements, so it is important for you to review every employee file, as a prudent seller will do the same.*

1b.   Review personnel files for other employee contracts/agreements as well as job descriptions.

1c.   Disclose if there are "golden parachutes" (bonuses certain employees receive upon being terminated when ownership changes) or other significant or unusual compensation arrangements.

1d.   Provide copies of any loan agreements between the business and any officers, employees, consultants, or members of the board of directors.

1e.   Provide copies of all indemnification agreements, contracts, or understandings involving the company.

2.   Provide a listing of all employees. For each employee, list:
- Name
- Date of hire
- Current salary including any bonuses
- Date of birth
- Job title
- Insurance coverage and share of premiums
- Exempt/nonexempt status
- Date and amount of last salary increase
- Accrued vacation, sick, and other compensatory compensation
- Demographics (age, sex, race)
- Indicate if any employee is related to another employee or to the owner of the company.

QUICK TIP

Every business should continually maintain and update this data in a spreadsheet or database.

3. Review all employment contracts, offer letters, and any other documents that relate to terms of employment.

4. Obtain a list of all consultants retained by the company. For each consultant, provide:

   - Contact information

   - Social security or federal identification number

   - Annual amounts paid over the past three years

   - Whether 1099 forms have been issued to the consultant/subcontractor

   - A copy of the agreement, if any, between the consultant/subcontractor and the company

5. Obtain a list of all sales representatives and distributors who sell products or services for or on behalf of the company or to whom the company pays commission or remuneration. For each entity listed, provide:

   - Contact information

   - Social security or federal identification number

   - Annual amounts paid over the past three years

   - Whether 1099 forms have been issued and a copy of any and all written agreements, if any, between the entity and the company

6. Disclose any personal or nonbusiness expenses paid by the business.

7. Assemble all documents regarding related-party transactions. This includes real estate rentals, loans, purchases, and sales.

8. Review all employee manuals and communications with employees.

9. Report the status and history of the business's labor relations.

10. Review any labor grievances and requests for arbitration. If applicable, review history of any strikes, work stoppages, or other actions.

QUICK TIP

Although an information technology business may not have experienced many of these events, any unusual change in your company's personnel may provide an indication of the business's overall organizational stability and management strength. The reasons for (and effects of) any layoffs should be analyzed.

11.   Review any labor and other collective bargaining agreements.

12.   Review personnel policies and practices, including human resources manuals.

QUICK TIP

These documents can provide a sense of the company's operating philosophy.

G. Benefit Plans and ERISA

1a.   Review all documentation for compensation, bonus, and incentive plans. Many companies have incentive plans, some of them oral. When preparing a business for sale, you should ascertain and fully document all compensation plans, written and oral.

1b.   For any oral plan, provide a written summary.

2.   For all qualified retirement and deferred-compensation plans, review:

- Plan documents
- Summary plan description booklets
- Financial statements and IRS and Department of Labor filings
- Actuaries' reports
- Insurance contracts
- Annual statements provided to employees
- Favorable determination letter, opinion, or ruling from the IRS for each benefit plan
- Listing of the names, contact information, and annual amounts paid to any retiree, alternate payee, spouse, or beneficiary over the past three years, by the retirement plans, the company, or a related entity

- Copies of any Qualified Domestic Relations Orders received by the company.

3. Review all plan documents and insurance contracts for any non-qualified plans as well as stock option and purchase plans.

H. REAL PROPERTY

All of the company's assets should be disclosed, including such nonbusiness ones as personal-use automobiles, boats, paintings/sculpture, and so on. *Try to determine, either formally or informally, the fair market value of these assets if they will be part of the sale.*

1. Obtain a list and description of all real property owned or leased.

2. For all company-owned properties, review:

   - Deeds

   - Surveys

   - Title insurance policies

   - Mortgages or other encumbrances

   - Zoning

3. Order title searches as appropriate and review reports of same.

4. Obtain leases, options, and amendments for all leased real estate.

5. Review any appraisal reports obtained or received on any assets owned by the company or any obligations owed by or to the company.

6. Review any land purchase or sale agreements, options to purchase or sell land, and building or construction contracts.

7. Determine if there are environmental issues on any of the properties.

I. PERSONAL PROPERTY

1. Prepare a list of all fixed assets and personal property owned by the business by location. (This includes all software licenses and any other intangible assets.)

2. For each asset, obtain and review:

   - Date of purchase

   - Purchase amount

- Fair market value

- Location

- Accumulated depreciation

- Any appraisals previously performed

- License

- Physical identification, which should be performed for all significant assets, to determine if those listed on the business's financial statements and supporting schedules exist, and if all actual assets are reflected on the business's financial statements and supporting schedules

3. Order and review state and county lien and judgment searches.

QUICK TIP

These searches will show if there are any liens or judgments recorded against the business or its assets.

J. INTANGIBLE ASSETS

1. List all patents, trademarks, service marks, and copyrights owned by the business and their federal and international documentation.

2. List all licenses and permits owned.

3. Review any appraisals or reports obtained on these assets.

4. Obtain copies of all applications for all patents, trademarks, service marks, and copyrights that have been submitted and are pending a determination.

K. CUSTOMERS AND SUPPLIERS

1. Prepare a schedule of major customers of and suppliers to the company and its subsidiaries, indicating:

- Materials and/or services supplied or purchased

- Nature of goods and services provided

- Contract termination dates

- Basic terms of contracts and agreements

- Detailed terms of contracts and agreements

2a. Provide copies of all material contracts, present or contemplated, to which the company is or will become a party, including but not limited to:

- Supplier contracts
- Customer contracts
- Sales pipeline and projections
- Sales backlog
- Leases
- Rental services agreements
- Warranties
- Licensing agreements
- Franchise agreements
- Agency or commission agreements
- Sales agreements
- Value-added resellers

QUICK TIP

If possible, you should memorialize or record all of these agreements in writing during the ordinary course of business.

2b. For each contract, review:

- Terms
- Assignability
- Pricing
- Constraints
- Warrantees
- Guarantees
- Performance standards
- Buyouts
- Unusual/extraordinary circumstances, such as one party's right to terminate or change the contract upon the sale of the business

3a. Provide a list of the company's customers, their location, and a summary of the services the company performs and products it sells for each as well as the annual sales to each customer over the past five years.

3b. Provide a list of the company's 10 largest customers as measured by annual revenues over the past five years.

3c. Provide a list of the new contracts, as opposed to renewals of ongoing contracts, sold per year over the past five years.

3d. Provide a list of the deconversions, or lost customers, per year over the past five years.

4. Provide copies of the company's sales compensation programs as well as any contracts between the company and its salespeople or outside sales representatives, if not previously provided.

5a. Provide samples of the business's current and prior marketing and sales literature.

5b. Provide a price list for the company's product and service offerings.

6. Obtain copies of all outstanding or pending proposals submitted to or received from existing or prospective clients or suppliers.

QUICK TIP

This requirement can include sales projections, or "pipelines," indicating the likelihood of prospective clients signing contracts and existing customers purchasing additional goods and services from the company.

7. Obtain copies of all contract forms used by the seller and its subsidiaries.

8. Provide a list of your competitors.

QUICK TIP

If you, the owner, and your management team appear to have a detailed understanding of the competition, you can impress potential buyers. Such knowledge indicates that you are savvy about the market(s) in which you operate. Include analysis of competitors' strengths and weaknesses in your business plan. However, you may not want to disclose this information to certain buyers until you are confident that their interest is genuine.

L. Tax Review

1. Provide the names and contact information for the business's certified public accountant(s) and other tax advisors.

2. Review copies of all business income, payroll, sales, use, and other required tax and government filings.

3. Review any pending tax audits, waivers of the statute of limitations, releases, offers in compromise or other documents executed or received in connection with any pending audits.

4. Obtain all revenue agents' reports, correspondence, communications, and notes for all pending, resolved, or potential federal, state, or local tax proceedings for open years or items relating to the company and its subsidiaries.

5. Search for any tax liens.

6. Review correspondence, bills, and statements from the CPA and other tax advisors.

Quick Tip

As with attorneys' itemized statements, a review of CPAs' and tax advisors' bills can provide valuable information concerning the business's operations.

7. Review the CPAs' work papers, files, correspondence, and so on.

Quick Tip

A company often is subject to taxation in multiple jurisdictions. The buyer will attempt to determine if all of the necessary tax filings have been made. This is an area that may also be covered in the seller's representations and warrantees.

M. Financial Review

1. Provide the name and contact information for all auditors retained by the business over the past five years along with copies of all invoices received.

2. Provide the business's financial statements for the past 10 years.

3. Internal management reports as well as all financial records of the
   company, including but not limited to:

   • General ledger

   • Sales journal

   • Disbursements journal

   • Receipts journal

   • Fixed asset schedule

   • Accounts receivable journal and aging schedule

   • Inventory workpapers

   • Accounts payable and accrued expense journal and aging schedule

   • Payroll journal/ledger

   • Capital expenditure schedule/projection

   • Outstanding purchase orders

   • Reconciliation between expenses on financial statement and tax
     return

   • A listing of the banks, account numbers, and balances of all ac-
     counts owned by the company

4. Provide correspondence between your lawyers and your outside
   auditors.

5. Supply reports ("management letters") of any independent auditors
   employed by the company relating to management and accounting
   procedures for the company and its subsidiaries.

6. Supply all projections, forecasts, and budgets prepared by or for the company and its subsidiaries.

7. Provide auditors' work papers and client correspondence.

8. Review the companies' accounting methods and policies as well as any changes to accounting methods and policies.

QUICK TIP

In addition to these reviews, buyers should be permitted to speak with your auditor(s), including those for prior years, if you have changed.

N. COMPLIANCE REVIEW

1. Conduct an antitrust review and prepare Hart–Scott–Rodino Act filings, if applicable.

2. Conduct an environmental audit.

3a. Review compliance with all applicable federal, state, and local regulations. This includes (but is not limited to) Occupational Safety and Health Administration, Food and Drug Administration, and Equal Employment Opportunity Commission as well as state and local regulations. Compliance with the IRS and other tax authorities was discussed previously.

3b. Provide copies of all reports filed with federal, state, and local governments not previously requested as well as any correspondence received from the government agencies concerning these reports and filings.

4. Review all permits, licenses, and governmental consents.

5. Review any correspondence with government agencies or regulatory bodies.

O. MISCELLANEOUS

1. Compile press releases issued by the company.

2. Collect published articles about the company.

3. Assemble speeches presented or articles written by any officer or director of the company.

4. Search relevant databases (on the Internet and elsewhere) to review any information a potential buyer is able to obtain.

5. If not already done, keep copies of all articles in which your company is mentioned, press releases, and any speeches or articles written or prepared by employees. Among other purposes, these files can demonstrate the effectiveness of marketing, advertising, and public relations expenditures. It is important to do a search on the company and its principals on the various Internet search engines.

6. Provide copies of all joint venture and partnership agreements in which the company is or will become a party.

7. Supply the most recent business license applications.

8. Assemble waivers or agreements canceling claims or rights of substantial value (other than in the ordinary course of business) and documents relating to material write-downs and write-offs of notes or accounts receivable (other than in the ordinary course of business).

QUICK TIP

The company's officers should be familiar with and current on all industry trends in this regard.

9. Speak with relevant trade groups and associations.

QUICK TIP

Often a buyer will contract trade groups and associations do this to gauge the trends in the market. It is helpful if you are known to these groups and if the influential people in these organizations are familiar with your company.

10. Review acquisition offers, proposals, and agreements for the purchase, sale, and/or disposition of assets or stock of the company.

11. Review all existing and prior joint venture agreements.

12. Supply a copy of the company's disaster recovery plan.

13. Provide copies of all technical, procedural, operating, and system manuals and documentation utilized by and/or prepared by the company.

14. Provide copies of any software audits or reviews performed by third parties.

15. Supply copies of any appraisals performed on the business at any time during the past five years.

16. Supply copies of any industry surveys, relevant articles, and white papers.

CHAPTER 17

Forms of Acquisition, Contract of Sale, Utilization of Attorneys and Certified Public Accountants

FORMS OF ACQUISITION

An acquisition can take three basic forms: (1) asset purchase, (2) stock purchase, and (3) merger. Each has legal, tax, accounting, and practical issues that should be considered. It is important that you obtain competent professional advice in this area.

Asset Purchase

For the buyer who wishes to choose specific assets to purchase and liabilities to assume, the asset purchase may be the most desirable form. Although the buyer may be able to avoid assuming certain liabilities in this scenario—such as tax obligations, pending lawsuits, or claims—the shield may be limited under the theory of successor liability. Courts have determined that the buyer may be responsible for some or all of these obligations, even when a transaction was structured as an asset purchase, in certain situations including if it was a *de facto merger,* there was an express assumption of liabilities by the buyer, or if the bulk sales law (if applicable) was not complied with.

In an asset purchase, the consideration can be cash, promissory notes, the purchaser's stock, or other property.

There are three disadvantages to an asset purchase.

1. It can be an expensive and arduous process to identify and prepare the necessary documentation to transfer title to the individual assets. Moreover, jurisdictions may impose taxes or fees on the transfer of such assets as real estate, tangible assets, and vehicles.

2. The transfer of the assets, which can include contracts, rights, permits, licenses, or leases, may not be possible without the approval of third parties, such as suppliers, customers, landlords, or government agencies. Sometimes these parties will be unwilling to approve the transfer or will approve it only if they receive a fee or other concessions. In some instances, third parties may use this opportunity to terminate a contract that is unfavorable to them. Any of these impediments can reduce the value of the business and have a direct impact on the sales price.

3. Asset sales may be subject to double taxation if the seller is a taxpaying entity, such as a C corporation. The sale is first taxable to the corporate seller and again when the seller distributes the proceeds to its shareholders, resulting in double taxation first on the corporate level and then to the shareholder. This problem may be mitigated if the seller is a non-taxpaying entity, such as a limited liability corporation (LLC), subchapter S corporation, or partnership. If the seller is a taxpaying entity (i.e., a C corporation), payments made pursuant to a noncompete agreement, employment contract, and/or consulting agreement may avoid double taxation if made directly by the buyer to a shareholder. Both Federal and State tax laws should be reviewed in these situations by tax counsel as these laws have numerous nuances.

Stock Purchase

Theoretically, a stock purchase can be a straightforward transaction: The buyer purchases sufficient stock of the target to achieve its voting power and value goals. Because the ownership of the target is the only aspect that is changed, the seller as an entity remains unaffected. The consideration for the seller's stock can be cash, promissory notes, the buyer's stock, or other property.

Because the buyer is purchasing the stock of the seller, all of the seller's assets and liabilities are included. However, because the seller remains a separate and distinct entity, the liabilities remain with the seller and are not transferred to the buyer.

A major advantage of a stock sale from the seller's perspective is that the sale proceeds may be subject to tax at capital gains rates, which are lower than ordinary income tax rates. In contrast, the post acquisition tax treatment to the buyer is less favorable in a stock purchase than in an asset purchase since the buyer generally has more opportunity to allocate the purchase price to depreciable or amortizable property in an asset purchase. This disadvantage can be ameliorated, in part, by making an election under Section 338 (h) (10) of the Internal Revenue Code where applicable.

Another disadvantage of a stock purchase is that some of the seller's minority shareholders may be unwilling to sell their stock, forcing the buyer to contend with them. In certain instances, a merger can be utilized to acquire control of the target even when there are minority shareholders who object to the deal. However, from a practical view, many buyers will not purchase a privately held business unless they can acquire all of the outstanding stock of the seller. In other cases the minority shareholders may be subject to a pre-existing obligation to sell in a shareholder agreement.

A third disadvantage of a stock purchase is that even though title to the actual assets is not transferred, many contracts, leases, and other agreements include change-of-control provisions that require third-party approval upon a sale of the business.

Merger

In a merger, all of the assets and liabilities of the target are transferred to the buyer (acquirer) by operation of state law. As with a stock purchase, a merger does not involve the transfer of specific assets or the assumption of specific liabilities. However, certain third-party approvals may be required to transfer such intangible rights as contracts, licenses, rights, and permits. Moreover, the transaction is performed in one step; there is no need for additional measures to obtain the minority interests, providing all necessary corporate action is taken.

There are several disadvantages to a merger. Unlike a stock purchase, in which the seller remains a separate and distinct entity from the buyer and the exposure to the seller's liabilities is limited to the buyer's investment, the acquiring company assumes all of the seller's (target's) liabilities. For this reason, most mergers are structured as a forward triangular merger or a reverse triangular merger.

A second disadvantage of a merger is that the dissenting minority shareholders typically have appraisal rights, which enable them to receive cash for their stock as opposed to participating in the merger.

There are four forms of mergers: (1) forward merger, (2) reverse merger, (3) forward triangular, and (4) reverse triangular merger.

In a forward merger, the acquiring company is the surviving entity. The shareholders in the target or selling company receive stock in the acquirer in exchange for their stock, and all of the target company's assets and liabilities are transferred to the acquirer. One requirement for the receipt of the acquirer's stock in this transaction to be tax-free to the target's shareholders is that at least half of the consideration they receive consists of stock in the acquirer. The non-stock portion of the consideration is typically taxable upon receipt, subject to installment reporting. Once again, competent legal and tax advice should be obtained.

One disadvantage of a forward merger is that the acquirer is now responsible for the target's liabilities. In addition, certain third-party approvals may be required to transfer various assets, contracts, leases, and so on.

In a reverse merger, the target is the surviving entity. The shareholders in the acquirer or buyer exchange their stock for shares in the company being acquired, which assumes all of the assets and liabilities of the buyer. This form of a merger has been used when a closely held business goes public by purchasing the stock in an inactive publicly held business.

The two other forms of mergers, forward triangular mergers and reverse triangular, are structured with a subsidiary of the buying company being utilized as the acquisition vehicle. In a forward triangular merger, the acquiring subsidiary survives; in a reverse triangular merger, the target survives.

For a merger or acquisition to be deemed a tax-free reorganization and receive tax-free treatment, the transaction must conform to certain nonstatutory requirements and comply with Section 368 of the Internal Revenue Code.

THE CONTRACT AND ITS COMPONENTS

After you have agreed in general terms on the conditions of the sale, whether it is orally or by execution of the letter of intent (see Chapter 15), the specifics will be spelled out in a contract of sale. The contract can take myriad forms depending on the structure of the sale—asset purchase, stock purchase, or merger—as well as a host of other items, such as whether the seller will be paid in full at closing, whether there will be an earn-out or some form of deferred compensation or payment, and so on.

This section provides you, the seller, with some guidance on what you can expect to be included in the contract, so you can be better prepared. This book is *not* designed to provide you with drafting tips for the contract. Your lawyer should do the drafting and/or review of the contract. It is essential, and should go without saying, that an experienced attorney must be retained to assist with this aspect of the transaction, if not in all the previous aspects.

Asset Sale versus Stock Sale

Asset Sale   If the deal is structured as an asset sale, the contract will include a listing of the assets that will be purchased and the liabilities that will be assumed by the buyer. The assets to be purchased can include, but are not limited to, cash, accounts receivable, work in process, unbilled time, inventory, equipment (computers, furniture, vehicles, etc.), leasehold improvements, real estate, intellectual property (IP), leases, prepaid expenses, income tax refunds, investments in other entities, and life insurance policies. Intellectual property is a broad category that includes, but is not limited to, goodwill, patents, trademarks, copyrights, service marks, customer lists, and URLs. The contract will also specify any liabilities that will be assumed by the buyer including, but not limited to, accounts payables, accrued expenses, prepaid revenues/deposits, salaries and wages payable, unused vacation and sick time owed to employees, taxes payable, mortgages and notes, lease obligations, amounts owed to retirement plans, environmental exposures, warranties, and contingent liabilities.

In an asset sale, the contract will provide an allocation of the purchase price to the various assets. A vital component to the structure of any deal is the allocation of the purchase price. Typically the buyer and seller will agree in the contract as to the allocation, for tax purposes. However, this is an area in which your advisors should be consulted regarding the legal, tax, and accounting ramifications. There are advantages to either the buyer or seller, depending on the allocation. Exhibit 17.1 summarizes the effects of different allocations and provides the tax treatment for assets acquired as part of a purchase of a trade or business.

EXHIBIT 17.1   TAX EFFECTS OF DIFFERENT PURCHASE PRICE ALLOCATIONS

	Seller	Buyer
Accounts Receivable	Ordinary gain or loss on the difference between the value, as allocated, and tax basis	Ordinary gain or loss on difference between collection and allocated value
Inventory	Ordinary gain or loss on the difference between the value, as allocated, and the tax basis	Ordinary gain or loss on the difference between the allocated value and the sale price
Building	Generally capital gain, however amounts previously deducted as depreciation may be taxed at higher rates.	Capitalize and depreciate
Land	Generally capital gain and may qualify for ordinary loss if held for more than one year in a trade or business.	Capitalize, but not depreciated
Personal Property This includes machinery, equipment, and furniture.	Recapture is taxed as ordinary income. The remaining gain, if any, is taxed at Capital Gains rates. If there is a loss it is taxed as an ordinary loss.	Capitalize and depreciate
Created Goodwill and Other Intangibles (see IRC 197 (d) below).	Capital Gain	Capitalize and amortize over 15 years
Purchased Goodwill that has previously been amortized	Recapture is taxed as ordinary income. The remaining gain, if any, is taxed at Capital Gains rates. If there is a loss it is taxed as an ordinary loss.	Capitalize and amortize over 15 years.
Non-Compete Agreement	Ordinary Income	Capitalize and amortize over 15 years
Consulting Agreement Employment Agreement	Ordinary Income but also subject to FICA Tax	Current deduction

Note: I.R.C. Section 197 governs the amortization of intangibles for tax purposes. Pursuant to I.R.C. Section 197(d) intangibles include a) goodwill, b) going concern value, c) workforce in place, d) business books and records, operating systems or any other information base, e) any patent, copyright, formula, process, design, pattern, know how, format or other similar item, f) any customer-based intangible, g) any supplier-based intangible, h) any license, permit, or other right granted by a governmental unit or an agency or instrumentality thereof, i) any covenant not to compete entered into in connection with an acquisition of a trade or business, and j) any franchise, trademark or trade name.

Note: Prior to entering into any transaction, you always should obtain competent legal, tax, accounting and financial advice as every business's circumstances are different and should be analyzed individually.

Stock Sale   If the deal is being structured as a stock sale, the contract will provide the number of shares of stock in the company that are being purchased.

Purchase Price

In an asset sale, a stock sale, or merger the contract will discuss the purchase price. The purchase price can be a fixed amount and/or include a contingent component that may be structured as an earn-out. The earn-out often is determined based on the business's future performance or other events that occur or cannot be calculated until after the date of the contract or closing.

Method and Terms of Payment

Regardless of the structure of the deal, the contract should discuss the method and terms of the payment of the purchase price. Among the alternatives are cash payments at closing, the seller receiving stock in the purchaser, the seller financing the purchase, or an earn-out.

If a substantial portion of the purchase price is being paid in the form of the purchaser's stock, in reality the seller is buying a portion of the purchaser. In such cases, the seller should perform appropriate due diligence on the purchaser. Similarly, the seller should perform due diligence on the buyer if there is seller financing or a substantial portion of the purchase price will be paid subsequent to closing either in the form of seller financing or an earn-out.

QUICK TIP

The seller should keep in mind that if the business is projecting substantial future growth, an astute purchaser may structure the sale with a significant portion of the purchase price being contingent on the business achieving the projected growth. These payments are frequently referred to as an earn-out.

The earn-out payments could be contingent on the business's future revenues, gross margin, profits, cash flow, or a host of other benchmarks. From the seller's perspective, it is important that the payments be easily verifiable and not subject to manipulation by the purchaser. For example, the seller typically would prefer the earn-out payments to be based on the business's gross revenues as opposed to gross margin, profits, or cash flow, because the purchaser can deduct various charges or items when arriving at these figures.

If any portion of the purchase price is payable subsequent to the sale, the agreement typically will discuss the amount due at closing, the interest rate on outstanding amounts, the payment amounts, and due dates for the future payments. It will also discuss any terms and conditions applying to the future payments.

QUICK TIP

If the buyer will be paying a portion of the purchase price after closing, it is imperative that the seller perform due diligence on the purchaser to determine its ability to meet this obligation.

If the seller is receiving an employment or consulting contract for work to be performed subsequent to the sale, those terms typically will be discussed in an employment contract or consulting agreement and usually will also be discussed in the contract.

Security

If the seller is not going to be paid in full at closing, it should obtain security, such as a personal guarantee, holding the stock in escrow, and/or the placing of a lien or mortgage on the business assets of the target and/or the acquirer.

Seller's Representations and Warranties

In the contract, the seller will be required to make various representations and warranties to the buyer. This is one of the most important and negotiated sections of the entire contract. The representations relate to acts that have already occurred, and the warranties relate to events that may occur in the future. Some of these representations and warranties include:

1. *Seller is properly organized and validly existing:* The buyer wants to ascertain that the seller is in good legal standing in all of the jurisdictions in which it operates.

QUICK TIP

If your business is not validly organized, it may not have the authority to enter into the proposed transaction. Often businesses that are validly organized neglect to file reports or other necessary documentation annually with their statement of incorporation/formation. After a few years of nonfiling, many states will revoke a business's charter. In many instances, the charter can be reinstated by paying all of the back fees plus late fees and a reinstatement fee. However, it is far easier and more prudent to make the necessary filings and pay the required fees on a timely basis when they are initially due.

2. *Governing documents have been disclosed:* The buyer would like to review your business's governing documents, articles of incorporation and bylaws for a corporation, or certificate of formation and operating agreement for an LLC, to determine if there are any unique requirements or items in the organizational documents that should be addressed prior to entering into the transaction.

3. *Seller's stock is validly issued:* This is another check on the seller that the buyer will perform to determine if the ownership has been issued properly, which will enable the shareholders/members or partners to ratify the proposed transaction. (The parallel term for "stock" is "membership interests" in an LLC and "partnership interests" in a partnership. See Exhibit 7.1)

4. *Seller(s) is (are) lawful owner(s) of the property, free and clear of all liens and encumbrances:* The buyer wants to determine that your company has good title to the property being sold without any claims by others. Indicia of ownership can include deeds for real estate, patents, copyrights or trademarks for intellectual property, evidence of development for IP that may not be registered, and bills of sale for equipment purchased. Searches of state databanks can disclose liens under the Uniform Commercial Code.

QUICK TIP

As previously discussed, it is essential that your company ensure registration of all of its intellectual property, which includes patents, trademarks, service marks, and copyrights.

5. *Seller has the authority to sign the contract and consummate the transaction.*

QUICK TIP

Approval is required by the business's shareholders/members/partners as well as your board of directors or managers. The business documents that are reviewed in response to the business's formation and organization may provide further guidance.

Typically required are a resolution and the minutes from a meeting of the board of directors (or board of managers if the entity is an LLC) and or a resolution and the minutes of the meeting(s) of the shareholders (or members if the entity is an LLC).

6. *The execution of the contract will not result in a default or conflict of seller's other obligations.*

QUICK TIP

Frequently loan agreements include a "due on sale" clause, which states that the loan is due at the time the business is sold. Franchise and other agreements may provide for the agreement to terminate if the business is sold. Lenders, franchisors, suppliers, landlords, and others may agree to waive this provision, but securing the waiver can take some time.

7. *All necessary third-party approvals have been obtained (lenders, landlords, government, etc.)*

QUICK TIP

Government approvals may take time to obtain, require the filing of an application and payment of fees as well as various other conditions. Other nongovernmental, third-party approvals usually take time and resources to obtain too.

8. *Financial statements are complete and correct in all material respects.*

QUICK TIP

This may be the most important and far reaching representation being made, as far as the buyer is concerned. An accurate and complete financial statement with all of the necessary footnotes provides the key information about a business. However, the financial statements may not disclose many nonfinancial issues about a business.

9. *There have been no material changes by the business since its last financial statement.*

QUICK TIP

This representation becomes more important as the time between the date of the financial statement and contract increases. However, even if there is a very short time period, this representation, in some form, usually will be requested.

10. *All tax liabilities have been disclosed and accrued. All returns have been correctly filed and all taxes due thereon have been paid.*

QUICK TIP

This representation takes on even greater importance for businesses that oper-ate in multiple jurisdictions and may not always file the necessary income, sales, or franchise or other tax returns.

11. *All assets (equipment) are in working order.*

QUICK TIP

Immediately prior to closing, the buyer may want to verify if the assets are in working order. If they are not, a reserve may be held at closing to cover the estimated cost of the repairs.

12. *Inventory is usable and in salable condition:* It is not obsolete or damaged.

QUICK TIP

Inventory is a vexing problem in the sale of any business, and especially so with IT businesses, in which hardware that is still usable but may quickly become virtually unsellable due to obsolescence. The contract should be spe-cific as to the requirements that need to be met.

13. *All contracts entered into by the seller have been disclosed (including leases).*

QUICK TIP

It is important for you to provide a complete list and copies of all contracts the business has entered into, including oral ones.

14. *All real estate owned and leased by the business is in good condition, not in violation of any governmental laws, and all liens have been disclosed.*

QUICK TIP

Regardless of whether the real estate is owned or leased, this is an important representation as it includes compliance with environmental and zoning laws. A similar representation will be requested if the business leases its real estate because, as a tenant, the business may be liable for any violations or the vio-lations could interrupt operations.

15. *All known environmental issues have been disclosed.*

> **QUICK TIP**
>
> *Due to the wide impact of environmental laws, every business should carefully ascertain its compliance with all environmental laws and take any necessary steps to remediate any violations or problems.*

16. *The business is in full compliance with all laws:* All approvals and permits have been received.

> **QUICK TIP**
>
> *This is a catch-all provision that can have a far-reaching effect.*

17. *There is no ongoing, threatened, or anticipated litigation that has not been disclosed.*

> **QUICK TIP**
>
> *This is a potentially broad and onerous representation. Ongoing, threatened, or anticipated litigation can become a very broad, encompassing term. In addition, you, the seller, may not know about threatened or anticipated litigation, as your employees may not have apprised you of oral or written threats that they have received. As a result, it may be prudent to limit this representation to the knowledge of the shareholders and corporate officers.*

18. *The seller will take all reasonable steps to assist in the transition:* This includes making the transition with customers, suppliers, and employees.

> **QUICK TIP**
>
> *It may be prudent to insist that the buyer delineates what steps he or she deems to be reasonable. In the alternative, or as a supplement, these obligations may be listed in the employment contract.*

19. *All warranties, guarantees, and indemnities received or given have been disclosed.*

The buyer will frequently insist on this clause because it can have wide and far-reaching ramifications on the business's operations as well as the risk being assumed by the buyer.

20. *All employees have been disclosed.*

An acquirer wants to ascertain that there are no additional employees other than those previously listed. Buyers often request that sellers advise them of any raises received by their employees over the past year or so. Of particular concern, naturally, would be raises that have been given or promised just before the acquisition.

21. *All insurance has been disclosed.*

The buyer's confirmation of insurance coverage is especially important if the policies are occurrence based as opposed to claims made.

22. *All brokers' and obligations for finders' fees to intermediaries have been disclosed.*

It is important to list all brokers and obligations for finder's fees in the contract and indicate who is responsible if an entity that is not listed makes a claim for commissions in the future.

23. *All employee benefit plans are in compliance with ERISA.*

The Employee Retirement Income Security Act (ERISA) is a federal law that sets minimum standards for pension and other employee benefit plans in private industry. ERISA laws are extremely complex and change frequently. Many businesses do not update their plans regularly. It also may be difficult for you, the seller, to make this representation because your staff may not have the requisite knowledge. Appropriate ERISA counsel should be retained.

24. *All statements in the documents provided are true.*

QUICK TIP

The contract can contain hundreds of pages of attachments, which are frequently copies of the business's records or schedules including contracts, lists of receivables and payables, employee census, employee salary, wage and bonus history. This representation, too, is very broad.

---

25. *An escrow is held to indemnify the buyer for obligations that cannot be determined or that arise after closing.*

QUICK TIP

Depending on the size of the transaction as well as the buyer's concerns and inclination, he or she may ask that an escrow be held by a third party to serve as a fund to pay any future claims. The seller should insist that there be a very strict limit on the period of time that the escrow is held and that there are minimum and maximum limits on the claim. The escrow agent should be identified in the escrow agreement and the requirements when the monies can be released are specifically delineated. A process such as arbitration should be followed in the event that the buyer and seller cannot agree whether an item is to be disbursed. It is important to obtain an impartial third party as the escrow agent although counsel to one of the parties is often used.

Buyer's Representations and Warranties

The agreement, regardless of the legal form of the transaction, will include the representations and warranties of the buyer, which are typically far less extensive than what the seller provides. However, more extensive representations may be appropriate in which there is a substantial deferred payment or the seller is receiving the buyer's stock as part of the deal. The buyer's representations and warranties can include that the buyer is validly and legally organized and existing, it has the authorization and approval to make the purchase, and the purchase does not violate any other commitment of the buyer. Typically the agreement will provide who is responsible for the payment of any fees to intermediaries, such as brokers, and transfer taxes.

Other Promises and Covenants

The agreement may also provide for any other promises made by the parties including, but not limited to, any noncompetition agreements made by the seller, its principals, owners, or employees. Some of these requirements include:

- The assignment of any rights, contracts, leases
- The manner in which the seller should conduct business between the time of contract and the actual closing
- Any conditions that are required for closing to occur, such as the receipt of government or other approvals, financing, documents to be provided by the parties prior to closing, such as the forms of notes, mortgages, deeds, titles, assignments, and so on
- The methods utilized to resolve any differences between the parties, such as arbitration, mediation, use of escrows
- A requirement that the agreement and its terms be kept confidential

QUICK TIP

Purchasers of businesses will almost always insist that key individuals execute noncompete agreements at the time the business is sold. Noncompete agreements can be very broad and typically cover a time period of one to two years, or longer, from the date of the transaction or from the date the individuals' employment with the company terminates. If the individuals being requested to sign noncompete agreements are shareholders (and hence will gain from the sale), often this is an item that can be negotiated. However, if the employees who are being asked to sign the noncompete agreements are not shareholders, these employees may require that they be compensated by either the buyer or the seller.

Regardless of who is being asked to sign these agreements, all persons should have their own counsel review them. As the selling owner, you and your advisors should attempt to discourage the buyer from being overly aggressive in asking nonshareholder employees to sign these agreements.

Seller's Promise to Indemnify Buyer

An important and extensively negotiated provision of the agreement usually will be the seller's promise to indemnify the buyer for any breach of representations and warranties. The agreement can define how losses are calculated and the responsibility of each party.

Although the buyer may want the seller to be responsible for all losses incurred subsequent to the date of closing, the seller will attempt to limit the scope of his or her indemnifications. For example, the seller's indemnifications can be limited to a period of time following closing and the seller may be liable for any losses but only after the total losses exceed a predetermined amount. Thereafter, the seller can be liable for all of the losses, beginning with the first dollar, or only for the losses above the predetermined amount. Or the seller may be responsible for a percentage of the losses and the buyer the balance. There can also be a maximum amount, or a cap, that the seller will have to pay to indemnify the buyer. Frequently the seller's obligation is based on the amount of the purchase price. Most buyers typically insist that the seller have no limit on the amount of indemnification that is paid resulting from losses from fraud or tax liabilities.

Concomitantly, most sellers often are reluctant to agree to indemnify the buyer for any losses incurred, because this promise transfers or converts a corporate obligation of the selling entity, which the seller typically satisfied from the business's cash flow during his or her ownership, to the seller individually. A buyer typically will request a personal guarantee for this indemnification.

Because the promise by the seller to indemnify the buyer is only as good as the person providing it as well as his or her financial resources, the buyer may request that a portion of the purchase price be held in escrow to be used to pay for any losses. The seller will want to limit the amount of the escrow and the period in which the funds will be held. Both parties should have the agreement provide for an escrow agent and the terms and conditions when the funds can be released and forwarded to the seller.

Buyer may also request that they have the right to reduce any payments that they normally would pay the seller by any amounts they are owed by the seller. This is referred to as set-off rights.

Moreover, there is frequently a provision to arbitrate any disagreements between the buyer and the seller as they relate to the use of the escrow funds and set-off rights. The agreement can specify where the arbitration will be held, who will be the arbitrators, or the qualifications of anyone who will serve as an arbitrator.

Miscellaneous Provisions

The agreement will also discuss the method of closing sale, either through escrow or by the means specified in contract. It will also discuss many miscellaneous provisions that are important and should not be overlooked. They can include:

- The responsibility to maintain the business's records
- An agreement for the parties to cooperate in the event there is an audit or litigation with a third party in the future
- Which party is responsible for various expenses incurred during and after the transaction
- Whether the contract can be assigned or not
- Whether the contract is binding on successor entities
- The process required to amend the agreement
- The requirements to notify each of the parties in the event there is a breach or need to contact the other party
- The jurisdiction whose laws will govern any disagreements between the parties and in which any disagreements will be litigated
- A statement that the contract is the entire agreement between the parties
- Whether the agreement can be signed in counterparts That is, can each party sign a separate copy of the agreement, as opposed to all parties signing the same copy or copies.

UTILIZING ATTORNEYS AND CERTIFIED PUBLIC ACCOUNTANTS

Every seller should retain an experienced commercial attorney to assist with the transaction and should utilize corporate counsel, assuming one exists, only as co-counsel. As seller, you may not realize that it is seldom in your company's best interests to use your corporate counsel as lead attorney if he or she is inexperienced in handling business sales. However, your long-standing corporate counsel can assist in components of the transaction and serve as co-counsel.

The lead attorney probably will need the services of lawyers who have expertise in a wide array of areas, including antitrust, intellectual property, tax, employee benefits, leases, real estate, and local laws. As no one individual will be knowledgeable in all of these areas, it is important to retain lawyers with experience in the relevant fields, either from the attorney's firm or through contacts.

Attorney's fees typically are based on time expended and expenses. In certain instances, law firms may agree to a flat fee for the transaction; however, this is less common.

You will undoubtedly need your business's certified public accountant to assist in the sale. The CPA's role can vary from responding to questions about the business's tax and accounting policies and procedures to preparing for the due diligence process and structuring the transaction. As with attorneys, CPAs typically are paid for time and expenses, or sometimes they negotiate a flat fee.

CHAPTER 18

After the Sale

The approach of closing can be a tumultuous, hectic, and emotionally draining time for you, the owner. During this period, your time frequently is consumed with operating the business, communicating with and providing data to the purchaser, and assisting with the business transition. As the business owner, you should be mindful that what you do—or do not do—during this period could have a profound effect on the success of the business and the sale. Moreover, as the owner, you should be mindful that it may be difficult to interact with long-term employees on a daily basis knowing they are unaware that the business that they have worked at for many years may be soon changing hands.

The sale of a business can fail or not achieve its full potential, for many reasons: The sale may occur at an inappropriate time, the buyer and/or the seller may not prepare sufficiently for the sale, the strengths and weaknesses of the employees may not considered, and/or the relationships between the business and its customers, suppliers, and industry may not be appropriately understood. Attention to all of these factors can help to improve the likelihood of success after the sale.

As has been discussed earlier in this book, there are numerous steps that you can take prior to the sale to increase the odds that the business will succeed. These four steps by the seller include:

1. Developing management and organizational depth
2. Fostering strong customer and supplier relationships
3. Building a manageable, but vibrant, order or work backlog
4. Generating a sustained demand for the business's offerings.

These steps should be performed well, and optimally years, in advance of the sale.

Besides their technology, IT firms' greatest assets include their employee base and their business relationships with suppliers and customers. Regarding the employees, both the buyer and the seller should be mindful that the business's success is dependent on the employees' efforts and overall job satisfaction. Prior to the sale, the seller should meet with the buyer to evaluate the employees and determine what should be done to harness their strengths, skills, and expertise. This should include meeting with the employees, if possible, evaluating job descriptions, redesigning compensation and incentive plans, and maintaining and improving the work culture and environment, while retaining the positive attributes of the business. Seemingly simple steps by the buyer such as improving the physical conditions of the office (i.e., purchasing new furniture and computers or remodeling the facilities), and listening earnestly to the employees' comments, concerns, and complaints can improve morale and productivity while reducing the likelihood of employee unhappiness and turnover.

Both the purchaser and the seller should keep in mind that just as they are evaluating the employees, the employees will be continually evaluating management's overall effectiveness and their vision for the business.

Employees frequently become unsettled after a sale due to changes in the work culture, the perception that the business is becoming more bureaucratic, and the general feeling that the new owner(s) do not understand the business or do not value their opinions. An unclear mission, changes in the business's strategy, or a different business model can fan the flames of discontent. Acts such as delaying the date of employee reviews, changing the health insurance carrier or the amount of the employees' health insurance deductible, altering the dress code, reducing the amount of vacations and holidays, or changing the work hours can damage employee relations. The purchaser should remember that, in many cases, the business was purchased because it was succeeding; changes should be made sparingly—at least initially.

In many instances, the purchaser can improve employee relations at a very low cost by maintaining popular attributes of the business's culture and altering the areas that cause the most discontent among the employees.

The purchaser should always give careful consideration to bolstering employee benefits and improving work conditions immediately after the purchase. Employee benefits or perquisites, such as expanded employer 401(k) matching contributions, discounted employer stock purchase programs (if the acquirer is publicly held), and awarding bonuses to key employees who remain with the business are frequently very successful. The purchaser may want to consider paying bonuses to employees who remain with the business for specified periods of time, such as six months or a year following the sale. However, the purchaser should seek the seller's guidance and advice regarding the structure of these initiatives and to whom they should be offered. Similarly, the purchaser should, with the advice of the seller, consider which employees should be offered lucrative assignments, enrolled in sought-after training programs, or be groomed for promotion.

Although it may sound contradictory, a business owner should plan on working at their former business for a period of time after the sale.

Although it is prudent for the seller to remain with the business immediately after the sale, it is rare for the sellers to still be employed by the new owners 18 months following the sale. Typically, the sellers do not enjoy working for someone else, are interested in pursuing other endeavors—either business or pleasure—or just may be tired of the business that they sold.

When informed of a sale, usually employees, customers, and suppliers alike will ask how the business will change. If the former owners are still working at the business and can speak with these groups, it will allay many of their concerns. Moreover, the mere presence of the key managers, along with the former owner(s) after the sale, diminishes the concerns of the business's most important constituencies: its employees, customers, and suppliers. After the sale, both the buyer and the seller should be available to answer employees' questions through a variety of forums, which can include individual and group meetings, telephone conferences, and e-mail. Moreover, an astute purchaser will structure the sale price to provide some monetary incentive for the sellers and/or their key managers to remain with the business after the sale and benefit if the business succeeds. The incentives should be designed to reward the sellers and/or key managers in areas where they exercise control and can make a difference.

QUICK TIP

*If the former owners' strengths are in the areas of maintaining customer rela-
tionships, they should receive additional compensation if these relationships
are maintained at certain levels or grow. Similar incentives should be imple-
mented if the seller's strengths are in sales, research and development, or any
other facet of the business.*

The purchaser should remember that the integration of the new business
will take time. However, the purchaser should be continually attentive to
employee requests, always respond promptly, and be candid. Employees
may not always agree with your answers; however, they should appreciate
your attentiveness.

The seller should also remind employees that although the business will
change after the sale, it would have to change over time anyway, even if the
business had not been sold, as all organizations change. Employees frequently have more opportunities for personal growth and advancement,
professional development, and increased remuneration at larger businesses.

Online Resources

The reader can obtain updates to this list by going to www.chalfin.com and clicking the "resources" button.

WHAT BUYERS ARE LOOKING FOR

www.allbusiness.com   This Web site provides thorough guides, resources, forms, and advice for all types of small businesses. The Web site is designed to provide practical solutions to real-world problems that occur with owning your own business.

www.asbdc-us.org   The Association of Small Business Development Centers is dedicated to providing educational assistance to small businesses. This Web site offers information on how to protect your business.

www.enterweb.org   The Small Business Portal serves as a database of information to guide the small business owner.

www.isquare.com   The Small Business Advisor is a Web site that is "dedicated to advising and assisting" small business owners. The advisors from this site are entrepreneurs themselves and have government experience.

www.itaa.org   The Information Technology Association of America is the leading trade association serving the IT industry. This Web site contains resources as well as links to other related sites.

www.morebusiness.com   This Web site provides a general overview of information covering most areas essential to the small business, from creating a business, to financial matters, to employee management and more.

www.nasbic.org   The National Association of Small Business Investment Companies is an organization that helps protect small businesses on a federal level.

www.NFIB.com   The National Federation of Independent Businesses is the largest organization representing small and independent businesses on a federal level. The purpose of this federation is to have a positive impact on public policy related to the businesses it represents.

www.nsba.biz   The National Small Business Association advertises itself as being America's Small Business Advocate. This Web site offers a broad range of information concerning small businesses.

www.nwen.org   The Northwest Entrepreneur Network provides information to the owner that the site finds necessary for success.

www.sba.gov   The United States Small Business Administration (SBA) offers government assistance and counseling for small businesses.

www.sba.gov/sbdc   The SBA provides a Web page specifically designed for a Small Business Development Center.

www.score.org   The SCORE Web site is run by retired executives, also known as the Counselors to America's Small Businesses. It offers a free exchange of advice on small businesses from experienced professionals.

www.startupjournal.com   The Wall Street Journal Center for Entrepreneurs offers a free resource for entrepreneurs to find information on running a business.

www.youngentrepreneur.com   Young Entrepreneur offers a wide variety of information guides, forums, forms, directories, and advice pertaining to the small business.

Why Sell?

www.bizhelp24.com   This Web site provides a general overview of the process of selling a small to medium-size business. It contains a range of information, from reasons to sell a business, to common mistakes made by the seller.

www.business.com   This Web site offers a search engine of services, companies, and news related to owning your own business.

www.business.gov/   This Web site provides information to help you understand government rules and regulations.

www.sellerworks.com   This Web site can be used as a resource to help guide a business owner in deciphering the process of selling

The Selling Memorandum

www.bizhelp24.com   This Web site offers a step-by-step guide to preparing a selling memorandum. The small business section is helpful.

www.businessplans.org   The Business Plan Center offers software that helps with writing a business plan and offers sample business plans. In addition, this Web site offers links and resources for other business planning information.

www.itssimple.biz   ItsSimple.biz provides a thorough description of how to prepare a selling memorandum as well as advice on owning your own business from experienced business owners.

www.smallbusinessplanguide.com   This Web site offers a wide variety of resources for entrepreneurs and small businesses. It also contains links to hundreds of other sites that provide small business resources.

Attracting and Retaining Key People

www133.americanexpress.com/osbn/tool/biz_plan/index.asp   American Express Small Business Plan Resources offers many resources, including advice on key personnel as well as general aspects of maintaining a small business

www.inc.com *INC Magazine* offers many articles pertaining to retention of personnel for your business.

FINANCIAL METRICS

www.bitpipe.com This site offers all the information needed to run an IT business, including explanations of different aspects. Search under "business metrics" to gain a better understanding of the term.

www.bizfsbo.com This site offers a different perspective on the process of selling a business. It gives a more realistic approach to determining the financial metrics of your business.

www.uschamber.com The United States Chamber of Commerce offers financial planning and advice on creating and maintaining a successful business.

YOUR BOARD

www.boarddirectorsnetwork.org This Web site is dedicated to increasing the number of women on boards of directors. It offers resources and networking tools.

www.corpgov.net This Web site offers news, links, and commentary to help aid corporate governance.

www.encycogov.com This Web site advertises itself as The Encyclopedia for Corporate Governance.

www.fdic.gov/regulations/resources/directors The Federal Deposit Insurance Corporation offers general guidelines for your board of directors to follow.

www.governanceinstitute.com This Web site, run by the Governance Institute, advertises itself as offering "unbiased governance knowledge."

www.managementhelp.org/boards/boards.htm This Web site, the Free Management Library, offers a "complete toolkit for boards" as well as links to other resources.

www.oecd.com The Organization for Economic Co-operation and Development offers "corporate governance principles" that can act as a guide.

www.wikipedia.com This Web site is free web based encyclopedia. Search for "corporate governance" and find an extensive resource list.

MARKETING YOUR BUSINESS FOR SALE

www.bizhelp24.com This Web site offers advice on different ways to market your business to reach the right buyers.

www.fortune.com/fortune/smallbusiness *Fortune Small Business*, a part of *Fortune Magazine*, gives continual advice to small businesses.

www.globalbx.com The Global Business Exchange features a forum for buying and selling businesses. It also provides a comprehensive listing of professional business brokers.

www.mergernetwork.com This Web site offers a marketplace for the purchase and sale of businesses of all industries and sizes. It also provides additional marketing options for selling your business.

Valuing Your Business: An Introduction

www.bvresources.com   Business Valuation Resources, LLC, offers a forum where you can ask questions related to the valuation of your business that will be answered by professionals or other members.

www.ebizbrokers.com   This Web site provides a description of the different ways to value your business to find the appropriate method of valuation for your business.

www.valuationresources.com   This Web site provides business valuation publications and resources. It also contains a broad list of links to other industry data relevant to valuing your business for sale.

Valuation: Company Value and Financial Condition

www.businessfinance.com   BusinessFinance.com advertises itself as being "America's Business Funding Directory." Its Web site contains information that will aid in the financing and financial status of the business.

www.entrepreneur.com   Entrepreneur.com advertises itself as having the "Solutions for Growing Businesses." Search for "business valuation" and you will find many articles that can be used in valuing a business.

www.smallbusinessnotes.com   Small Business Notes offers a wide range of resources for small businesses, from how to set up a profit and loss statement to marketing your business.

Methods of Determining a Business's Value

www.appraisers.org   The American Society of Appraiser's Web site offers guides for beginning the business appraisal process provided by professional business appraisers.

www.bvresources.com   The Business Valuation Resources Web site strives to give the user the necessary information to compile a valuation.

www.mergerstat.com   This site provides merger and acquisition information to the corporate financial marketplace.

www.score.org   SCORE, which was created and maintained by retired executives, features articles that give the basic facts to value a business.

Confidentiality: An Introduction

www.allbusiness.com   This is the place to go if you need sample forms (including a confidentiality agreement) and some advice for your business. This site serves the small business owner.

CONFIDENTIALITY: LIMITING DATA DISSEMINATION AND PREPARING CONFIDENTIALITY AGREEMENTS

www.amstat.org   The American Statistical Organization provides legal documents that reference confidentiality. Search for "confidentiality."

www.coollawyer.com   CoolLawyer.com offers an overview of confidentiality from a legal perspective and answers the most frequently asked questions.

www.investopedia.com   This site offers information on a wide range of topics. You can search the dictionary and be provided with a definition and related links, or click on articles or research tabs for more in-depth answers. Here you can find information relating to valuation, confidentiality, due diligence, letters of intent, and many other topics.

www.nolo.com   Nolo describes itself as being "the leader in do-it-yourself legal solutions for small businesses." This Web site also offers resources such as forms, checklists, articles, and a dictionary on business terminology.

www.toolkit.cch.com   This site answers many of the business owner's how-to questions. It provides short explanations for everything from starting your business to exiting. It also explains the process of confidentiality.

LETTER OF INTENT

www.allbusiness.com   This is the place to go for sample forms (including a letter of intent) and some advice for your business. This site serves the small business owner.

www.alllaw.com   AllLaw.com offers an enormous database for just about everything legal. For example, this Web site offers information, from a legal perspective, on the items needed in a thorough letter of intent.

www.investopedia.com   This site offers information on a wide range of topics. You can search the dictionary and be provided with a definition and related links, or click on articles or research tabs for more in-depth answers. Here you can find information relating to letters of intent and many other topics.

www.jurisint.org   Juris International features different examples of letters of intent as well as a search engine for other small business resources.

www.toolkit.cch.com   This site answers many of the business owner's how-to questions. It provides short explanations for everything from starting your business to exiting. It also explains the necessity of a letter of intent.

DUE DILIGENCE

www.allbusiness.com   This is the place to go for sample forms (including a due diligence checklist) and some advice for your business. This site serves the small business owner.

www.investopedia.com   This site offers information on a wide range of topics. You can search the dictionary and be provided with a definition and related links, or click on articles or research tabs for more in-depth answers. Here you can find information relating to due diligence and many other topics.

www.toolkit.cch.com This site answers many of the business owner's how-to questions. It provides short explanations for everything from starting your business to exiting. It also explains the process of due diligence.

www.urgentbusinessforms.com This Web site provides a description of each of the forms required for the sale of your business. You can also purchase forms from this site.

The Contract of Sale

www.allbusiness.com This is the place to go for sample forms (including sales contracts) and some advice for your business. This site serves the small business owner.

After the Sale

www.allbusiness.com This is the place to go for sample forms and some advice for your business. This site serves the small business owner. Many articles explain what to do after you have sold your company.

Other Sites of Interest

Databases of Businesses for Sale

www.bbn-net.com The Broker's Network Group offers business sales by experienced business brokers and intermediaries.

www.BeTheBoss.com BeTheBoss is a database of businesses and franchises for sale.

www.BizBuySell.com BizBuySell is the largest business-for-sale exchange. It has over 30,000 active businesses for sale.

www.BizForSell.com This Web site offers an exchange forum for the buying or selling of businesses. It also offers advice on the valuation of your business.

www.bizplanit.com BizPlanIt is a consulting firm that helps companies develop business plans. This Web site offers free business plan data.

www.bizQuest.com This Web site is a marketplace for the purchase or sale of a business. It also offers resources to purchase your business online.

www.businessresale.net Business Resale's Web site contains a database for the purchase and sale of businesses, but it also has resources specific to the type of business for sale.

www.Franchise.org The International Franchise Association's Web site is the place to start if you are looking for information on franchises. Whether you want to buy, sell, or maintain the franchise, this site has the tools to steer you in the correct direction.

www.FranchiseDirect.com Franchise Direct offers a directory of franchises and resources to improve your franchise

www.IdeaCafe.com Idea Café: Small Business Help offers information on how to start and run your business.

Business Valuation Resources

www.appraisers.org   The American Society of Appraisers offers discussion forums as well as business valuation resources.

www.smbiz.com   The Small Business Taxes and Management's Web site provides tax and management help to the business owner.

www.toolkit.cch.com   The CCH Business Owner's Toolkit offers a small business guide as well as an "Ask Alice" column that offers advice for small businesses.

Government-Provided Data

www.bbb.com   The Better Business Bureau provides resources for on over 2 million organizations, which will help you make a well-informed investment.

www.bls.gov   The Bureau of Labor Statistics Web site offers publications such as the *UC Occupational Outlook Handbook*.

www.bos.frb.org   The Boston Federal Reserve Bank Web site.

www.business.gov   This Web site provides information to help you understand government rules and regulations.

www.cbo.gov   The Congressional Budget Office Web site.

www.census.gov   The U.S. Bureau Census Web site.

www.census.gov/statab/www   The U.S. Bureau Census offers a *Statistical Abstract of the United States* at this Web site.

www.chicagofed.org   The Chicago Federal Reserve Bank Web site.

www.dallasfed.org   The Dallas, Texas, Federal Reserve Bank Web site.

www.doc.gov   The Department of Commerce Web site.

www.economicindicators.gov   Economic indicators sponsored by the Economics and Statistics Administration.

www.federalreserve.gov   The Board of Governors' Web site offers government information on the economy and the central banking system. There are also links to the 12 other Federal Reserve Bank's Web sites.

www.federalreserve.gov/releases   The Web site for Federal Reserve Statistics releases.

www.fedworld.gov   FedWorld is a program sponsored by the U.S. Department of Commerce.

www.firstgov.com   The U.S. Government's official Web portal.

www.frbatlanta.org   The Web site of the Atlanta Federal Reserve Bank.

www.frbsf.org   The Web site of the San Francisco Federal Reserve Bank.

www.irs.ustreas.gov   The Web site of the Internal Revenue Service.

www.kansascityfed.org   The Web site of the Kansas City Federal Reserve Bank.

www.minneapolisfed.org   The Web site of the Minneapolis Federal Reserve Bank.

www.ny.frb.org   The Web site of the New York Federal Reserve Bank.

www.phil.frb.org   The Web site of the Philadelphia Federal Reserve Bank.

www.rich.frb.org   The Web site of the Richmond Federal Reserve Bank.

www.sba.gov   The Web site of the United States Small Business Administration.

www.sec.gov   The Web site of the Securities and Exchange Commission.

www.ssa.gov   The official Web site of the Social Security Administration.

www.stlouisfed.org   The Web site of the St. Louis Federal Reserve Bank.

www.whitehouse.gov/fsbr/esbr.html   The Web site of the Economic and Statistics Briefing Room.

Investing and Corporate Information

http://finance.yahoo.com   The Yahoo finance Web site.

www.10kwizard.com   10k Wizard, SEC Power Search Web site.

www.americanexpress.com/homepage/smallbusiness.shtml   The American Express Small Business Web site.

www.amex.com   The American Stock Exchange Web site.

www.BigCharts.com   BigCharts offers graphs of recent and historic economic data.

www.Bloomberg.com   The Bloomberg Web site.

www.bonds-online.com   This Web site offers access to coverage of stocks, securities, and several other fixed-income investing options.

www.briefing.com   This Web site offers unbiased analysis of the current stock market.

www.BusinessNation.com   The *Business Nation* Web site.

www.BusinessWeek.com   The *Business Week* Web site.

www.dnb.com   Dun & Bradstreet offers credit advice as well as business credit reports.

www.Economy.com   The Economy.com Web site.

www.edgar-online.com   This Web site offers business and financial information on global companies.

www.finpipe.com   This Web site offers a thorough introduction to the world of investing.

www.fool.com   *The Motley Fool* Web site.

www.forbes.com   The *Forbes Magazine* Web site.

www.fortune.com   The *Fortune Magazine* Web site.

www.ft.com   The *Financial Times* Web site.

www.fundalarm.com   This Web site offers advice on when to sell a fund rather than when to buy one.

www.hoovers.com   The Hoovers Online Web site.

www.ibbotson.com   The Ibbotson Associates Web site.

www.internetnews.com   The *InternetNews* Web site offers news for IT business owners.

www.INVESTools.com   The *INVESTools* Web site.

www.investors.com   The *Investor's Business Daily* Web site

www.Morningstar.com   The Morningstar Web site.

www.nasdaq.com   The NASDAQ Web site.

www.newsalert.com   The *MarketWatch* Web site.

www.nyse.com   The New York Stock Exchange Web site.

www.nytimes.com   *The New York Times* Web site.

www.PCQuote.com   The *PCQuote* Web site.

www.Quicken.com/small_business   The Quicken Web site.

www.quote.com   This Web site provides current stock quotes.

www.ReportGallery.com   This Web site provides annual reports.

www.ResearchMag.com   The *Research Magazine* Web site.

www.SmartEconomist.com   This Web site provides insights into economics, finance & business research.

www.SmartMoney.com   The *SmartMoney* Web site.

www.TaxFoundation.org   The Tax Foundation Web site.

wc ww.USAToday.om   The *USA Today* Web site.

www.wsj.com   *The Wall Street Journal* Web site.

Index